Early Acquisition of
Chinese Modal Verbs

汉语儿童情态动词
早期习得研究

杨 贝 著

科学出版社

北 京

图书在版编目(CIP)数据

汉语儿童情态动词早期习得研究＝Early Acquisition of Chinese
Modal Verbs/杨贝著. —北京：科学出版社，2014.6
ISBN 978-7-03-040966-9

Ⅰ. ①汉… Ⅱ. ①杨… Ⅲ. ①汉语-儿童语言-助动词-研究
Ⅳ. ①H193.1

中国版本图书馆 CIP 数据核字（2014）第 127355 号

责任编辑：阎 莉 常春娥／责任校对：刘亚琦
责任印制：钱玉芬／封面设计：刘可红

联系电话：010-64019007 电子邮箱：changchune@mail. sciencep.com

科学出版社 出版
北京东黄城根北街 16 号
邮政编码：100717
http://www. sciencep. com
双青印刷厂印刷
科学出版社发行 各地新华书店经销

*

2014 年 6 月第 一 版 开本：A5（890×1240）
2014 年 6 月第一次印刷 印张：7
字数：300 000
定价：68.00 元
（如有印装质量问题，我社负责调换）

前　言

情态动词被一些学者称作"困难词语"，这是因为，情态动词的语义是抽象的、多义的、复杂的，而情态系统中词与词之间语义的区别又是十分微妙的，因此，对于儿童而言，这些词是较难习得的。同时，情态也是儿童语言习得研究领域中一个很有趣的话题，这是因为通过研究情态的习得，我们可以获取有关儿童的语义发展以及社会发展和认知发展的重要信息。目前有关英语情态习得的研究比较丰富，而有关汉语情态习得的研究则一直处于比较薄弱的态势，急需全面、系统而深入的描述与考察。

本专著的研究总目标"汉语情态动词的早期习得研究"被具化为五个紧密相连的研究问题：（1）在儿童话语中情态词形呈现怎样的发展特征？（2）在儿童话语中三种情态语义类型呈现怎样的发展特征？（3）在儿童话语中情态句的句法结构呈现怎样的发展特征？（4）在成人话语中情态词形、情态语义以及情态句的句法结构分别呈现怎样的发展特征，这些特征跟儿童话语中的相应特征有何关系？（5）汉语情态动词早期习得受到哪些因素的制约，而这些因素又是以怎样的方式互动的？

为了回答上述研究问题，本研究采用自然观察法，通过日记、录音和录像这三种方式收集一个儿童芊芊1岁4个月到3岁3个月期间在自然状态下与看护者之间的自发语料，调查了汉语情态动词的早期习得状况。本研究调查的目标情态动词是："想""会""要""敢""愿意""能""可以""该""用""得"和"喜欢"。

对儿童情态词形习得的研究表明，情态动词在儿童1岁8个月到2岁4个月之间开始习得，"想"是最早习得的情态动词，随后，"会""要""敢""用""愿意""能""可以""该""得"和"喜欢"逐渐习得。情态动词的习得顺序与其使用频率呈现相关性，早习得的情态动词的使用频率也比较高，例如，情态动词"想""会"和"要"不仅习得得早，而且其使用频率也非常高。

对儿童情态语义习得的研究表明，动力情态和道义情态比认识情态早习得，芊芊于 1 岁 8 个月产出第一个表达动力情态意义的语句（"想"），于 1 岁 9 个月产出第一个表达道义情态意义的语句（"妈妈不要写"），于 2 岁产出第一个表达认识情态意义的语句（"姑姑该走了"）。情态语义类型的习得顺序与其使用频率呈现相关性，动力情态和道义情态不仅较早习得，其使用频率也较高，而认识情态不仅较晚习得，其使用频率也极低。

对儿童情态句句法习得的研究表明，情态句的句型呈现出逐渐多样化的趋势，芊芊最早产出的情态句是回答大人问话的简单的陈述句，随后开始产出完整的自发的陈述句，2 岁开始产出是非疑问句，随后产出选择疑问句和特指疑问句。此外，情态句的句法结构也呈现出逐渐复杂化的趋势，芊芊最早产出的情态句是单个的情态动词，从 1 岁 9 个月开始情态动词的前项能出现某些修饰副词，主要是否定副词"不"，除此之外，还有范围副词"都""只"，重复副词"还""也"，时间副词"现在""准备""立刻"，语气副词"才""就""肯定""非得"等，从 1 岁 9 个月开始情态动词的后项带动词和动词短语，从 2 岁 5 个月开始后项带"把"字句。

对看护者输入的研究表明，语言输入和儿童情态习得之间存在动态的、双向的关系。一方面，输入频率高的情态词形以及情态语义类型会较早习得，例如，"想"和"会"被习得之前在输入中的使用频率均为 18%，这两个词也最早习得；动力情态被习得之前的输入频率为 55%，动力情态最早习得。另一方面，情态习得也会对语言输入产生一定的影响。情态句在儿童话语和输入中都显示了逐步增多的趋势，此外，情态句在输入中的百分比一直都比在儿童语料中的百分比要高一些，这说明看护者会随着儿童情态习得的发展逐步增加情态输入，使输入既能够被儿童理解又能够促进儿童下一个阶段的语言发展。

汉语情态动词的习得特征与以下三种因素都有关系：情态系统本身的复杂性、儿童的心智发展、成人的语言输入。只有综合考虑这三种因素的动态互动，才能够充分解释习得过程呈现的特征。例如，认识情态较晚习得可能是源于以下三种因素的共同作用。首先，认识情态在语义上更加抽象。动力情态和道义情态分别表达存在于自然界和社会中的可能性和必然性，而认识情态则表达存在于心理世界的可能性和必然性，后者比前者的语义更加抽象。其次，认识情态对儿童的认知水平要求较高。认识情态表达对事件为真的可能性判断，与对信念的理解有关，儿童只有意识到信念和事实可能会不同，而且信念的确定程度又有高低之分，他们才能够开始习得认识情态。最后，认识情态被习得之前在输入中的使用频率只有 5%。以上三种因素的综合作用导致了认识情态较晚习得。

本研究是迄今为止对汉语情态动词早期习得进行系统研究的第一本著作，在数据收集方法和研究思路上具有一定的创新性。首先，鉴于不同的数据收集方法各有优劣，同时使用日记、录音和录像收集数据可以为语言习得研究提供更全面、更可靠的证据。其次，母语习得是一个动态的复杂的过程，研究者只有综合考虑语言项目自身的特征、输入特征和儿童的认知发展水平等多种因素及其动态交互，才能够充分解释这一过程。然而，由于儿童语言习得研究具有一定的复杂性，且作者水平有限，对许多问题可能研究得不够，不足之处敬请专家和读者指正。

杨 贝

2013 年 2 月

Acknowledgements

I would like to extend my deepest gratitude to Prof. Dong Yanping, who has shared with me the joys and sorrows of every step of the project. Prof. Dong is a precise and profound thinker, who is always generous with her ideas. She has spent countless hours reading and re-reading the manuscripts, helping me reformulate my raw and chaotic ideas into logical argumentations.

I would like to thank Prof. Wu Xudong, Prof. Wang Chuming, Prof. Zheng Chao, Prof. Huo Yongshou and Dr. Wang Wenxin for helping me clarify my ideas as well as encouraging me to pursue interesting new intellectual horizons. Without their time, patience, and wisdom, this monograph would have been filled with even more imperfections than it currently contains.

I am grateful to all the members of the psycholinguistic group, Zhao Chen, Li Guangze, Zhang Qunxing, Wei Hang, Cai Rendong, Lin Jiexuan, Zhao Nan and Yan Hao, for their interest and suggestions throughout the project. Their friendship and assistance have made this special journey easier and more enjoyable.

I am also grateful to the 30 juniors in Guangdong University of Foreign Studies majoring in linguistics who helped me transcribe the audio and video materials. Their hard work has saved lots of time for me. The many questions asked by them have also prompted me to think deeper about language acquisition.

For providing financial support, I would like to thank Guangdong University of Foreign Studies, and School of English and Education. My heartfelt thanks are also expressed to Ms. Yan Li and Ms. Chang Chun'e who arranged the publication of this book.

I owe a great deal to my husband, my daughter, my mother and other family members. My husband Hu Chunyu has offered a willing ear and sage advice from the beginning of the research and has kept part of the diary notes. My daughter Qiān Qian has been very cooperative when she was treated as an experiment subject, although she may not have known it at that time. She has also been very understanding when she was sent away to live with her grandmother so that her mother could concentrate on writing. Thank you, Qiān Qian, I dedicate this monograph to you. I could not have finished the monograph without the encouragement and help from my mother, Zhao Fuzhi, who has been very helpful whenever needed. I am forever grateful and indebted to her for her passionate love, hearty support, and selfless sacrifice. I would like to thank all the other family members for their constant love and support.

Contents

前言 ······i

Acknowledgements ······v

Chapter 1   Introduction ······1

1.1   Research Orientation ······1
1.2   Rationale ······1
  1.2.1   The Importance of Modal System ······1
  1.2.2   The Importance of Modal Acquisition in Child
      Language   Research ······2
  1.2.3   The Deficiency of Previous Studies on Chinese
      Modal   Acquisition ······3
  1.2.4   Summary ······5
1.3   Scope ······6
1.4   Organization of the Book ······7

Chapter 2   Modal Acquisition ······8

2.1   Modality ······8
2.2   English Modal Auxiliaries ······9
2.3   Chinese Modal Auxiliaries ······10
  2.3.1   Terms and Modal Forms Proposed by Chinese Linguists ······10
  2.3.2   The Syntactic Characteristics of Chinese Modals ······12
  2.3.3   The Semantic Characteristics of Chinese Modals ······20
  2.3.4   The Pragmatic Characteristics of Chinese Modals ······36
2.4   The Acquisition of Modality ······38
  2.4.1   Previous Studies of Modal Acquisition in English and
      Other Languages ······39
  2.4.2   Previous Studies of Modal Acquisition in Chinese ······53

2.5   Theoretical Accounts of L1 Modal Acquisition ···················· 56

    2.5.1   Perkin's Explanation ·· 56

    2.5.2   The Theory of Mind Hypothesis ·························· 57

    2.5.3   Caregiver Input and Acquisition of Modality ·············· 60

    2.5.4   A Converging Constraints Model ······················· 62

2.6   Research Questions ·· 63

2.7   Summary ··· 64

Chapter 3   Methodology ··· 66

3.1   Case- study Methodology ····································· 66

    3.1.1   Defining Case Study ·· 66

    3.1.2   Advantages and Disadvantages of Case Study ············· 67

    3.1.3   Justification for the Application of Case Study Method ········· 70

3.2   The Subject and Settings ······································ 71

3.3   Data-collection Procedures ···································· 71

    3.3.1   The Handwritten Diary ····································· 72

    3.3.2   The Audio-recordings ······································ 73

    3.3.3   The Video-recordings ······································ 74

3.4   Data Transcription and Analysis ······························ 74

Chapter 4   Features of Modals in the Child's Data and in the Caregivers' Data ································· 81

4.1   The Acquisition of Modal Forms in the Child's Data ·············· 81

    4.1.1   The Emergence of Chinese Modal Forms in the Child's Data ······· 81

    4.1.2   Distribution of Modal Forms in the Child's Data Across Time Periods ·· 90

    4.1.3   Summary ·· 94

4.2   The Acquisition of Semantics of Modals in the Child's Data ······· 95

    4.2.1   The Semantic Category of Modals for the First Occurrence in the Child's Data ·· 95

    4.2.2   Distribution of Semantic Categories of Modals in the Child's Data Across Time Periods ································· 98

4.2.3   Summary ···113

4.3   The Acquisition of Syntactic Structures of Modal
Utterances in the Child's Data ·· 114

4.3.1   Distribution of Syntactic Structures of Modal Utterances
in the Child's Data Across Time Periods ···························114

4.3.2   Sentence Types and Semantic Categories of Modals in the
Child's Data···121

4.3.3   Subjecthood and Semantic Categories of Modals in the
Child's Data···122

4.3.4   Summary ···124

4.4   A Comparison of the Features of Modals in the Caregivers'
Data and in the Child's Data Across Time Periods ·············· 125

4.4.1   Distribution of Modal Forms in the Caregivers' Data and
in the Child's Data Across Time Periods ···························125

4.4.2   Distribution of Semantics of Modals in the Caregivers'
Data and in the Child's Data Across Time Periods ·············130

4.4.3   Distribution of the Syntactic Structures of Modal Utterances
in the Caregivers' Data and in the Child's Data Across
Time Periods ···147

4.4.4   Summary ···154

Chapter 5   General Discussion ··· 158

5.1   Summary of Major Findings ··· 158
5.2   Discussion·· 159

References ··· 164

Appendix   The First Five Occurrences of Modals
in the Child's Data ·· 176

List of Tables

Table 1-1 The linguistic means to express modality ⋯⋯⋯⋯⋯⋯ 6

Table 2-1 Semantic categories of Chinese modals ⋯⋯⋯⋯⋯⋯ 21

Table 3-1 Time periods of audio and video recordings ⋯⋯⋯⋯⋯ 75

Table 4-1 The first occurrence of Chinese modal forms in the child's data ⋯⋯⋯⋯⋯⋯⋯⋯⋯⋯⋯⋯⋯⋯⋯⋯ 83

Table 4-2 The first occurrence of main verb uses of target forms in the child's data ⋯⋯⋯⋯⋯⋯⋯⋯⋯⋯⋯ 87

Table 4-3 The child's production of utterances and modal utterances between 1; 4 and 3; 3 ⋯⋯⋯⋯⋯⋯⋯ 91

Table 4-4 Distribution of modal forms in the child's data across time periods ⋯⋯⋯⋯⋯⋯⋯⋯⋯⋯⋯⋯⋯ 93

Table 4-5 Distribution of the semantic categories of each modal form in the child's data across time periods ⋯⋯⋯⋯ 103

Table 4-6 Distribution of the semantic categories of each modal form in the child's data ⋯⋯⋯⋯⋯⋯⋯⋯⋯ 104

Table 4-7 Age of the first occurrence of interrogative constructions in the child's data ⋯⋯⋯⋯⋯⋯⋯⋯⋯ 116

Table 4-8 Sentence types and modal categories in the child's data ⋯⋯⋯⋯⋯⋯⋯⋯⋯⋯⋯⋯⋯⋯⋯ 122

Table 4-9 Subjecthood and modal categories in the child's data ⋯⋯ 122

Table 4-10 Distribution of modal utterances in the caregivers' data across time periods ⋯⋯⋯⋯⋯⋯⋯⋯⋯ 126

Table 4-11 Distribution of modal forms in the caregivers' data and in the child's data across time periods ⋯⋯⋯⋯⋯ 127

Table 4-12 Distribution of the semantic categories of each modal form in the caregivers' data and in the child's data across time periods ⋯⋯⋯⋯⋯⋯⋯⋯⋯⋯⋯ 134

Table 4-13 Distribution of the semantic categories of each modal
form in the caregivers' data and in the child's data·········136
Table 4-14 Sentence types and modal categories in the caregivers'
data and in the child's data···151
Table 4-15 Subjecthood and modal categories in the caregivers'
data and in the child's data···153

List of Figures

Figure 4-1   The semantic category of modals for the first
occurrence in the child's data ·· 96

Figure 4-2   Distribution of modal categories in the child's data
across time periods ··· 99

Figure 4-3   Distribution of modal utterances in the caregivers'
data and in the child's data across time periods ············ 126

Figure 4-4   Distribution of modal categories in the caregivers'
data across time periods ··· 131

Figure 4-5   Distribution of dynamic modals in the caregivers'
data and in the child's data across time periods ············ 132

Figure 4-6   Distribution of deontic modals in the caregivers' data
and in the child's data across time periods ···················· 132

Figure 4-7   Distribution of epistemic modals in the caregivers'
data and in the child's data across time periods ············ 133

Figure 5-1   A dynamic interactive model of contributing factors
on modal acquisition ·· 159

Abbreviations and Symbols

AUX	Auxiliary
ASP	Aspect
CL	Classifier
CONJ	Conjunctive
D	Diary
DE	Deontic modals
DY	Dynamic modals
EMP	Emphatic
EP	Epistemic
P	Particle
p	Proposition
PHA	Perfective phase marker
PRON	Pronoun
rpt	Reprinted
*CHI	utterance by the child
*MOT	utterance by the mother
*FAT	utterance by the father
*GRM	utterance by the grandmother
*GRF	utterance by the grandfather
%act	accompanied actions with the utterance
@Comment	comments to the utterance
xx	unintelligible speech, treated as a word
#	short pause between words
##	long pause between words

Chapter 1

Introduction

1.1 Research Orientation

The present study is intended to investigate the emergence and early development of Chinese[1] modality of a single child Qian Qian (Q hence). It is based on the longitudinal analyses of the naturalistic productions of Q between 1; 4 to 3; 3[2]. More specifically, it attempts (1) to explore the ontogenesis of Chinese modality in Q's utterances and to what extent Q's data accord to the same pattern of modal acquisition that has been well recorded in the literature; (2) to give a unified account of the observed patterns, if any, and to explore how these factors interact at different stages of modal acquisition.

1.2 Rationale

1.2.1 The Importance of Modal System

Modality is an important area of language. The ability to communicate through language is a benchmark of human competence. There appears to be two basic uses to which language is put: "we can use language either to comment on, or assert, our representation of the world, or else to effect some changes in the world through the mediation of other agents" (Perkins 1983: 12). Thus Austin (1962) distinguishes between 'constative' and 'performative' utterances;

---

1 This study is directed at Mandarin Chinese.
2 1; 4 means 1 year and 4 months old; 3;3 means 3 years and 3 months old.

Halliday (1973) between the 'ideational' and 'interpersonal' macro-functions of language. Modal expressions, because they encode the attitudes (or judgments) speakers take toward the proposition that describes the event, are essential to the two basic functions of language. Consider, for example, a proposition like

(1) 他 在 办公室.
Tā zài bàn gōng shì.
he at office
'He is in his office.'

With the addition of a modal such as 会 huì 'may', 可能 kěnéng 'may', 不可能 bù kěnéng 'can't', speakers can make a variety of judgments about the proposition, from expressing their degree of certainty, through probability and possibility, to impossibility. Similarly, if speakers add a modal obligator such as 得 děi 'must', 应 该 yīnggāi 'should', 可以 kěyǐ 'able to', to the proposition,

(2) 你 去。
Nǐ qù.
you go
'You go.'

the utterance will function very differently, from strong obligation (or an order), through weak obligation (or suggestion), to permission.

1.2.2 The Importance of Modal Acquisition in Child Language Research

Modality is an intriguing topic in child language research because it is a domain that can give us important information about children's semantic, social and cognitive development. As Nuyts (2006) puts it, modality refers to some kind of qualification of state of affairs. This means that by using modal expressions, speakers state more than just what they see: with modal forms speakers can add their own or other people's psychological or mental states regarding the proposition. Accordingly, when children acquire a set of modal expressions, they have grasped at some level the notion that a proposition can be qualified to include their own or other people's assessment about it. Guo (1994: 5) states that to seek to understand the acquisition of modality is to set out on a fascinating voyage of discovery in children's mind. Studies of emergence and early development of modal auxiliaries may provide us with a window for children's cognitive, psychological and social-interactive world in general, since modal auxiliaries express notions such as desire, volition, ability, permission, obligation, and logical possibility and necessity.

1.2.3   The Deficiency of Previous Studies on Chinese Modal Acquisition

Children begin to use modality relatively early, when they are about 2 years old, while children of 12 years old or even older come to fully acquire the adult modal system (Coats 1988), especially as far as the epistemic uses[1] of modality are concerned. Researchers have carried out naturalistic studies as well as experimental studies to explore the development of modality. The naturalistic longitudinal studies on the acquisition of modals mainly focus on the order of appearance of modal forms, the semantic aspects or the syntactic aspects of modal acquisition. The experimental studies mainly examine some detailed aspects of the way children acquire epistemic modal meanings as well as children's ability to distinguish differences among modal meanings. Naturalistic studies agree that, in general, children start acquiring modals around 2; 0; epistemic modals are usually acquired after dynamic and deontic ones; and early modals

---

1 Linguists usually group modality into three categories: dynamic modality, deontic modality and epistemic modality. Dynamic modality and deontic modality are classified as root modality. See chapter two for a detailed description of modality.

mainly appear in simple declaratives (Brown 1973; Stephany 1979, 1986; Wells 1985; Shatz and Wilcox 1991; Papafragou 1998, etc.). Experimental studies agree that children start developing epistemic notions from about 3 years of age, and that the greater the distinction in strength between two modal terms, the younger the age at which a distinction is reliably made (Hirst & Weil 1982; Coates 1988; Moore, Pure & Furrow 1990; Bassano Hickmann & Champaud 1992; Champaud, Bassano & Hickmann 1993). Researchers have proposed various accounts for the patterns of modal acquisition discovered, such as children's cognitive development (Perkins 1983), the theory of mind hypothesis (Gopnik & Astington 1988; Papafragou 1998; Moore, Pure & Furrow 1990, etc.), caregiver input (Wells 1979; Shatz, Grimm, Wilcox, et al. 1990; Choi 1991, 1995, etc.), a converging constraint model (Shatz & Wilcox 1991), etc.

In contrast to the rich literature on the acquisition of English modality, literature on the acquisition of Chinese modality is scarce. There are only two studies available till now. In her study of the early acquisition of Chinese syntax by four children in Taiwan, Erbaugh (1982) reports that children start to use modal auxiliaries 会 huì 'know how to' and 要 yào 'want' between 1; 10 to 2; 4, and the two modals remain rare except in answer to adult questions. During 2; 6 to 3; 2, most of the full range of available modal auxiliaries appear in spontaneous declarative speech. These include not only 会 huì 'know how to' which is the only common modal during 1; 10 to 2; 4, but also: 能 néng 'can', 可以 kěyǐ 'may', as well as 敢 gǎn 'dare' and 应该 yīnggāi 'should'. The most frequently used form is 要 yào 'want' at that time.

Guo (1994) studied the syntactic forms, semantic meanings, and discourse functions of eleven Chinese modal auxiliaries in the speech of three groups of children aged 3, 5 and 7 years old respectively. The modals investigated are: 会 huì 'know how to, may', 能 néng 'can', 可以 kěyǐ 'able to, may ', 想 xiǎng 'desire', 要 yào 'want, must', 喜欢 xǐ *huan* 'like', 愿意 *yuàn yì* 'willing', 敢 *gǎn* 'dare', 该 *gāi* 'should', 得 *děi* 'have to, must' and 用 *yòng* 'need to'. His study discoverd that three-year-olds primarily focus on notions of personal ability and desires as a means for social dominance, and consequently use dynamic modal auxiliaries most frequently; five-year-olds focus on notions of permission and obligation, with deontic modal auxiliaries being most frequent in their speech; At age 7, interests in logical reasoning start to emerge, accompanied by the use of epistemic modal auxiliaries.

Studies on the acquisition of Chinese modality have provided some evidence for the patterns of modal acquisition that have been well recorded in the literature, i.e. modals emerge around 2; 0, and the first modals emerged expressed ability (会 *huì* 'know how to') or intention (要 *yào* 'want'). There are gaps, however, between the studies on the acquisition of modality in Chinese and those in English. Discussions on the acquisition of Chinese modality by Erbaugh (1982) are very brief, which occupy only about two pages in her doctoral dissertation, thus leaving lots of questions unanswered. The sequence of acquisition of modals, the semantic and syntactic features of the modals and the factors constraining the acquisition of modals are left untouched. Guo's (1994) study was a cross-sectional investigation with the youngest group aged 3 years old, which made it impossible to discover the emergence and early development of modality.

To overcome the drawbacks of previous studies, we carry out a longitudinal study on one child from 1; 4 to 3; 3 to investigate the emergence and early development of Chinese modal acquisition and to explore the factors constraining the acquisition process.

1.2.4　Summary

Studies on the acquisition of English and other languages show that children begin to acquire modality toward the end of the second year and they acquire root modalities before epistemic modalities. Studies also suggest that early modal forms are more semantically and pragmatically motivated than syntactically driven. Compared with the ample studies on the acquisition of modality in English, only two studies on the acquisition of Chinese modality are available till now (Erbaugh 1982, Guo 1994). These two studies are either too cursory (Erbaugh) or missed the important period before 3 years old (Guo 1994), so that many important developmental patterns concerning modality acquisition were not discussed at all. To overcome the drawbacks of previous studies on the acquisition of Chinese modality, the present study aims to investigate the acquisition of modality by one child in detail, which is the first systemic study on the emergence and early development of Chinese modality till now. The present study is significant in that (1) it attempts to explore the emergence and early development of modal verbs in Q's utterances between 1; 4 to 3; 3 and (2) it ventures to propose a unified account to explain early development of modal verbs as displayed in Q's data.

1.3   Scope

Modal meanings can be expressed in several ways, such as main verbs, adverbs, intonation, modal verbs, particles, and nouns as illustrated in Table 1-1. The focus of this investigation is on modal verbs.

Table 1-1   The linguistic means to express modality

	Means	Examples
1	Main verb	Main verbs, such as 打算 *dǎsuàn* 'plan', 希望 *xīwàng* 'hope', 相信 *xiāngxìn* 'believe', 认为 *rènwéi* 'consider', etc., implicitly express modal meanings of probability of occurrence assessment. For example, 我认为他是对的。*Wǒ rènwéi tā shì duì de*. 'I think he is right'.
2	Adverb	也许我错了。*Yěxǔ wǒ cùo le*. 'Perhaps I'm wrong.'
3	Intonation	A sentence uttered with a rising intonation at the end may mean that the speaker is not certain of a state of event. E.g. 他生病了。*Tā shēngbìng le*. 'He is sick.'

Continued

	Means	Examples
4	Modal verb	下这么大雨，他会来吗? *Xià zhème dà yǔ, tā huì lái ma?* 'It's raining heavily. <u>Will</u> he come?' 大蒜能杀菌。*Dàsuàn <u>néng</u> shā jūn.* 'Garlic <u>can</u> disinfect.'
5	Particle	In Chinese, uncertainty or advice may be suggested by particle, a monosyllabic item with no independent meaning of its own but serving to deliver a structural or functional message when placed at the end of sentence e.g. 他好像是这么说的吧。*Tā hǎoxiàng shì zhème shuō de <u>ba</u>.* 'That's what he said, it seems.'
6	Noun	没有必要再讨论了。*Méiyǒu <u>bìyào</u> zài tǎolùn le.* 'There is no <u>need</u> to discuss it any more.'

(Adapted from Li 2003: 2)

1.4   Organization of the Book

The book consists of 5 chapters, which are structured as follows.

Chapter 2 reviews relevant literature from four aspects: (1) the concept of modality; (2) the English modal system and the Chinese modal system; (3) previous studies on L1 modal acquisition; and (4) theoretical accounts for the acquisition of modality.

Chapter 3 first describes and verifies the case study method adopted in the present study, and then specifies the subject and settings, data-collection procedures, data transcription and analysis procedures.

Chapter 4 presents findings of the present study: (1) the developmental pattern of Chinese modal forms in the child's data; (2) the developmental pattern of the three semantic categories of Chinese modals in the child's data; (3) the developmental pattern of the syntactic structures of modal utterances in the child's data; (4) the pattern of modal uses in the caregivers' data with respect to the formal, semantic, and syntactic characterization of modal utterances.

Chapter 5 discusses factors affecting L1 modal acquisition.

Chapter 2

Modal Acquisition

This chapter surveys the literature on modality and its acquisition. 2.1 examines the concept of modality, which is followed by a description of the syntactic, semantic, and pragmatic aspects of the modal system in English and Chinese in 2.2 and 2.3 respectively. Section 2.4 reviews previous researches on modal acquisition in English and Chinese. Theoretical accounts proposed for the acquisition of modality are provided in section 2.5. The last section 2.6 briefly summarizes the whole chapter.

2.1 Modality

Modality concerns the speaker's 'attitude' toward the content of what he is saying, including obligation, necessity, permission, volition, intention, ability, possibility, certainty, etc. Although such attitudes may sometimes be expressed in verbs, adverbs, and other forms, it is the grammaticalized forms that have received the most research attention.

Linguists usually group modality into three categories, namely dynamic modality, deontic modality, and epistemic modality (Palmer 1986). Dynamic modality refers to possibility and necessity in the natural world. It includes physical power and ability and psychological state like wishes and desires. Deontic modality refers to possibility and necessity in the social world, which includes social or moral obligation and rights, and permission and prohibition.

Epistemic modality refers to possibility and necessity in the mental world as in the process of human reasoning.

2.2   English Modal Auxiliaries

There are several ways to express modality in English, including modal auxiliaries such as *can*, modal adverbs such as *maybe*, complement- taking verbs such as *think* and *suppose*, etc. The most important devices, however, are the modal verbal constructions, including modal auxiliaries and semi-auxiliaries. In English the set of modal auxiliaries includes *can, could, may, must, might, should, ought, will*, and *would*. These words are defined as a set not only because they express related meanings but because they share a set of grammatical properties. A modal has the following characteristics (Chomsky 1957; Huddleston 1976; Palmer 1979; Coats 1983):

(1) a. Inversion with the subject (e.g. *Must he come?*)

b. Negative form with –n't (e.g. *He can't come.*)

c. 'Code' (e.g. *He will come and so will she.*)

d. Emphatic affirmation (e.g. *He May come.*)

e. No-*s* form of the 3rd person singular. (no * *mays*, * *cans* etc.)

f. No non-finite forms (infinitives, past and present particles).

g. No co-occurrence. (no * *he may will come* etc.)

The first four of these are so-called the NICE properties and they draw very clearly a dividing line between auxiliaries and main verbs. The last three, which are specifically 'modal' criteria (Palmar 1979: 9), are needed to exclude the auxiliaries BE, HAVE and DO. Palmer (1990: 4) admits that not all modal verbs conform to all of these criteria. WILL, SHALL, MAY, CAN, MUST and OUGHT TO fit all the criteria with the exception that MAY has no-*n't* form in the present. MUST differ from the others in having no past-tense forms.

In addition, a set of semi-modality, *hafta, wanna, gonna, gotta, and needta,* which express similar meanings and which share some but not all of the grammatical properties of "true" modality, are often considered along with them in discussions of English modal expressions (Garcia 1976).

Although modals cannot combine with tense, they can combine with marked aspect and voice:

(2) a. A virus air filter has been developed which *can be fitted* by the exhaust outlet. (modal with passive voice)

b. Well it *would have been* easier. (modal with perfect aspect)

c. This *has got to be moving* around this way. (modal with progressive aspect)

Some English modals are polysemous, for example, *can* can be a dynamic modal expressing ability in (3a), a deontic modal expressing permission in (3b) and an epistemic modal expressing possibility in (3c):

(3) a. They say Bill can cook better than his wife. (Quirk, Greenbaum, Leech, et al. 1985: 222)

b. In the library you can take a book out and keep it out for a whole year unless it is recalled. (Palmer 1990: 103)

c. It can't be there.— Oh, yes, it can. (Palmer 1990: 61)

2.3 Chinese Modal Auxiliaries

Showing a sharp contrast to the English modal auxiliaries which are relatively clearly distinguished from main verbs, Chinese lacks such explicit surface criteria and presents a complex situation for the formal identification of modal auxiliaries.

2.3.1 Terms and Modal Forms Proposed by Chinese Linguists

Since the publication of Ma' Grammar in 1898, the first Chinese grammar in Chinese linguistic history, Chinese modals are described under different names by different linguists, for example, 助动字 *zhùdòngzì* 'auxiliary verb' (Ma 1898; Li 1924; Ding 1953; Chao 1968; Li & Thompson 1981, etc.), 判断限制词 *pànduàn xiànzhìcí* 'restrictives for judgment' (Lü 1942), 能愿式 *néngyuàn shì* 'optative form' (Wang 1944), 能词 *néngcí* 'possibility words' (Gao 1948) etc. Of all the proposed terms, 助动词 *zhùdòngcí* 'auxiliary verb' is the earliest and one of the most popularly-used one (Li 2003: 109), while in recent years modal verb is a term often adopted by linguists (Tsang 1981; Alleton 1984; Yip & Rimmington 1997; Li 2003; Peng 2005, etc.), and this term will be used in the present study.

Chinese modals are a controversial set of linguistic forms. There are no two grammarians who have presented the same list of modals. Wang proposes 能愿式 *néngyuàn shì* 'optative form', and defines it as the sentence which mainly expresses speaker's attitude and will (Wang 1943 [rpt 1985: 75]). He (1942 [rpt 1985: 26]) states that Chinese has no category of auxiliary verbs like that in English, and further argues (p. 28) that Chinese words do not distinguish parts of speech in form and can, therefore, be categorized exclusively in terms of conceptual notions. Wang's list of optative forms include: 善 *shàn* 'be good at', 值得 *zhíde* 'be worth', 宁可 *níngkě* 'would rather', 想要 *xiǎngyào* 'would like to', 情愿 *qíngyuàn* 'would rather', 可能 *kěnéng* 'may'. His definition is too loose since the notion of modality may be expressed not only by modal auxiliaries, but also by full verbs, adverbs and adjective.

Chao's (1968: 731-748) 'auxiliary verb' includes the following forms: 要想 *yàoxiǎng* 'want to', 该当 *gāidāng* 'should', 必得 *bìděi* 'must', 好意思 *hǎoyìsi* 'have the cheek to', 懒得 *lǎnde* 'don't feel like to', 省得 *shěngde* 'save the trouble of' and 乐得 *lède* 'readily take the opportunity to'. Li and Thompson's (1981: 183) 'auxiliary verb' consists of the following forms: 应当 *yīngdāng*, 应该 *yīnggāi*, 该 *gāi* 'ought to, should'; 能够 *nénggòu*, 能 *néng*, 会 *huì*, 可以 *kěyǐ* 'be able to'; 能 *néng*, 可以 *kěyǐ* 'has permission to'; 必须 *bìxū*, 必要 *bìyào*, 必得 *bìděi*, 得 *děi* 'must, ought to'; 会 *huì* 'will, know how'; 敢 *gǎn* 'dare' and 肯 *kěn* 'be willing to'. Although Chao (1968) and also Li and Thompson (1981) take the same term 'auxiliary verb', their uses are very different. Li (2003: 130) notes that Chao's (1968) 'auxiliary verb' is a general term for both modal auxiliary verbs and other types of auxiliary verbs, whereas Li and Thompson (1981) use the term to refer to modal verbs exclusively.

Yip and Rimmington (1997: 85) use the term 'modal verb' instead of 'auxiliary verb', and treat modal verbs together with attitudinal verbs (e.g. 喜欢 *xǐhuān* 'like', 同意 *tóngyì* 'agree', etc.) and intentional verbs (e.g. 打算 *dǎsuàn* 'plan', 准备 *zhǔnbèi* 'prepare', etc.), since all these three types of verbs can precede the main verb in a sentence and can be negated. Generally speaking, Yip and Rimmington's modal verbs are similar to Li and Thompson's auxiliary verbs (Li 2003: 131). The forms proposed by Yip and Rimmington include all the forms identified by Li and Thompson except 应当 *yīngdāng* 'should', 必得 *bìděi* 'must', and 必要 *bìyào* 'necessity', and forms such as 要 *yào* 'want', 想 *xiǎng* 'miss', 愿意 *yuànyì* 'be willing to', 不用 *búyòng* 'don't have to', 不必 *búbì* 'need not' which are not included in Li and Thompson's list.

Guo (1994) studied the use of eleven modal verbs by Chinese children aged 3, 5, and 7 years old respectively: 会 *huì* 'know how to, may', 能 *néng* 'can', 可以 *kěyǐ* 'may', 想 *xiǎng* 'desire', 要 *yào* 'want, must', 喜欢 *xǐhuan* 'like', 愿意 *yuànyì* 'willing', 敢 *gǎn* 'dare', 该 *gāi* 'should', 得 *děi* 'have to, must' and 用 *yòng* 'need to'. Since Guo's study was the only reference available when the present investigation started, the eleven modal forms proposed by Guo, therefore, are the focus of this research.

2.3.2 The Syntactic Characteristics of Chinese Modals

Let us now look at the criteria suggested for modals by Chinese linguists. For the sake of clarity, the criteria will be numbered chronologically with Roman numerals first, and afterwards comments and criticisms will be made regarding the criteria mentioned.

Chao's (1968) criteria for his 助动字 *zhùdòngzì* 'auxiliary verbs' and comments on his criteria

Chao (1968: 731-733) proposes the following criteria for the classification of 'auxiliary verbs':

[i] An auxiliary verb occurs before a full verb.

[ii] Verbs can be reduplicated, but an auxiliary verb cannot. The following examples are not acceptable: 能能 *néngnéng* 'can can', 会会 *huìhuì* 'can can', 可可 *kě kě* 'may may' (example from Li 2003: 115).

[iii] Auxiliary verbs cannot combine with the particles of 了 *le*, 着 *zhe*, 过 *guò* (which indicate progressive aspect and perfect phase in Chinese). In other words, they do not allow the construction 'Aux+*le/zhe/guo*+V'. It would be ridiculous to say: 会着唱 *huì zhe chàng* 'can ASP sing', 能过唱歌 *néng guò chàngē* 'can PHA sing', and 肯了来 *kěn le lái* 'be willing to PHA come' (example from Li 2003: 115).

[iv] An auxiliary verb cannot take an object which is a 体词 *tǐcí* 'entity word'. In other words, it allows the construction 'Aux+V+N', but not 'Aux+N'. For example, 肯下棋 *kěn xià qí* 'be willing to play chess' is an acceptable sentence, whereas 肯棋 *kěn qí* 'be willing to chess' is not (example from Ding et al. 1953: 89).

[v] An auxiliary verb takes 不 *bù* 'not' in negation (24a). 没 *méi* 'not' applies in a restricted way to auxiliary verbs (24b) (Chao 1968: 731). This feature can be represented by '*bù*+Aux'.

(4) a.他　不　能　去。(Chao 1968: 731)

　　　Tā　bù　néng　qù.

　　　he　not　can　go

　　　'He cannot go.'

b. 他　昨儿　　没　能　来。(Ibid)

   Tā　zuó'er　méi　néng　lái.

   he　yesterday　not　can　come

'He could not come yesterday.'

[vi] The adverb of degree 很 *hěn* 'very' can be used with most auxiliary verbs (Chao 1968: 732).

(5) 这个　　时候,　我　很　　可能　　走上　　自杀的　路。

   Zhège　shíhòu, wǒ hěn　kěnéng　zǒushàng zìshā de　lù.

   this　time,　I　very may　follow　suicide P road

'At that time, I was liable to take my own life.' (*Home*《家》1)

[vii] Auxiliary verbs cannot be used to form imperative sentences.

(6) *能！(Chao 1968: 733)

   Néng!

   Can.

[viii] A Chinese auxiliary verb can have a positive-negative question form of the type 'Aux+bù+Aux' as in:

(7) 能　不　能　走　　啦？(Chao 1968: 735)

   Néng bù néng zǒu　la?

   can　not can　go　P

   'Can　I　go now?'

There are the following problems and exceptions with the criteria listed by Chao (1968).

Li (2003: 124) points out that the problem with [i] (auxiliaries occur before a full verb) is that Chinese auxiliary verbs can occur before main verbs as well as before adjectives, since Chinese adjectives can behave exactly like full verbs when serving as the predicate in a sentence. As in:

(8) 情绪　　要　热烈,　头脑　须　冷静。

Qíngxù yào rèliè,   tóunǎo xū lěngjìng.
attitude must enthusiastic, head necessarily calm
'Attitude must be enthusiastic, but brain calm.'
(Fan, Du & Chen 1987: 93)

Li (2003: 125) notes that [ii] (verbs can duplicate, while auxiliaries cannot) and [iii] (auxiliaries cannot co-occur with aspect markers) are problematic too. Some full verbs e.g. 成为 *chéngwéi* 'become', 等于 *děngyú* 'be equal to', and 当作 *dāngzuò* 'regard as', can not duplicate, and can not co-occur with aspect/phase markers 过 *guò*, 了 *le*, or 着 *zhe* (Liu, Pan & Gu 1983: 97). Therefore, these two criteria cannot distinguish auxiliaries from full verbs.

Li (2003: 125) states that [iv] (i.e. '*Aux+N') is not applicable to forms like 能 *néng* 'can', 会 *huì* 'can', 该 *gāi* 'should', 得 *dé/de* 'can', 应 *yīng* 'should', 要 *yào* 'must', 愿意 *yuànyì* 'be willing to', 喜欢 *xǐhuān* 'like', etc. When the above forms are followed by a full verb or adjective, they may be auxiliaries; when followed by a noun, they are full verbs. They should not be excluded from the category of auxiliary verbs because of their full verb status.

[v] (the use of 不 *bù* 'not' or 没 *méi* 'not' in negation) is not a feature for auxiliaries alone, but for almost all the verbs (Liu, Pan & Gu 1983: 94). Therefore, this criterion can show that auxiliaries belong to verbs, but it cannot distinguish between auxiliaries and verbs in general.

[vi] states that auxiliary verbs can be modified by 很 *hěn* 'very'. Li (2003: 128) points out that the pre-modification use of 很 *hěn* is restricted to those forms which indicate possibility and willingness such as 能 *néng* 'can', 可能 *kěnéng* 'may', 值得 *zhíde* 'worth', 可以 *kěyǐ* 'may', while the forms of other notions usually cannot be modified with 很 *hěn*. 很 *hěn* is more often used with adjectives, adverbs, and full verbs, e.g. 很高 *hěngāo* 'very high', 很快 *hěnkuài* 'very fast', and

很支持 *hěn zhī chí* 'very much support'.

[vii] rejects the imperative use of auxiliaries. Li (2003: 128) states that this point is true not only for auxiliaries, but also true for many full verbs, e.g. 种植 *zhòngzhí* 'plant' and 珍惜 *zhēnxī* 'treasure'.

[viii] states that a Chinese auxiliary can be used in the positive-negative construction 'Aux+*bù*+Aux'. But Hu and Fan (1995: 249) do not think this is true with the forms 应 yīng 'should', 得 dé/de 'can', 必 bì 'certainly', 须 xū 'necessarily', 必须 bìxū 'necessarily', 将 jiāng 'will', 可 kě 'may', and 怕 pà 'I'm afraid'.

Li and Thompson's (1981) criteria for their 助动字 *zhùdòngzì* 'auxiliary verbs' and comments on their criteria

Li and Thompson (1981: 172-182) suggest a much more refined set of syntactic criteria for the identification of Mandarin modals, and discuss their syntactic properties in comparison with main verbs and adverbs.

In Li and Thompson's system, auxiliary verbs share two distributional properties with the main verbs:

[ix] An auxiliary verb can have a positive-negative question form of the type 'Aux+bù+Aux' construction.

[x] An auxiliary verb may be negated:

But auxiliaries differ from main verbs in the following features:

[xi] An auxiliary verb must co-occur with a verb (or an "understood" verb). For example, (9) is incomplete and can be used only in a context in which a verb representing what he/she can do is understood:

(9) 他　能。
　　 Tā　néng.
　　 he　can

'He can.'

[xii] An auxiliary verb does not take aspect markers.

[xiii] An auxiliary cannot take a direct object.

[xiv] An auxiliary verb can not be modified by intensifiers, such as 很 hěn 'very' or 更 gèng 'even more'.

(10) *他　很(更)　　　　能　　唱歌。
  Tā　*hěn (gèng)*　　*néng*　*chànggē.*
  he　very (even more)　can　sing

[xv] An auxiliary verb can not be nominalized.

(11) *他　是　能　　的。
  Tā　*shì*　*néng*　*de.*
  he　be　can　NOM

[xvi] An auxiliary cannot occur before the subject.

(12) *能　　他　唱歌。
  Néng tā　*chànggē.*
  can　he　sing

As adverbs in Mandarin typically occur in pre-verbal positions like the auxiliary verbs, Li and Thompson proposes some test frames for the distinction between auxiliaries and adverbs.

[xvii] An auxiliary may be used in the Aux-not-Aux question construction as shown above, while adverbs cannot:

(13) *你　肯定　　　不　　肯定　　　来?
  Nǐ　*kěndìng*　*bù*　*kěndìng*　*lái?*
  you definitely　not　definitely　come

[xviii] An auxiliary may occur independently in elliptical sentences like main verbs, while adverbs cannot:

(14) Qu: 你　能　不　能　来?

　　　　Nǐ néng bù néng lái?

　　　　you can not can come

　　　　'Can you come?'

An: 我　能。

　　Wǒ néng.

　　I　can

　　'I can.'

Qu: 你　一定　来　吗?

　　Nǐ yídìng lái ma?

　　you definitely come QU

　　'Are you definitely coming?'

An: *我　一定。

　　Wǒ yídìng.

　　I　definitely

There are the following problems with the above criteria proposed by Li and Thompson.

The problem with [ix] is that some modals cannot pass the 'Aux+bù+Aux' construction, as has been discussed above. Furthermore, the positive-negative question form holds true not only for auxiliaries and full verbs, but also for adjectives, such as 好不好 *hǎo bù hǎo* 'good or not', 快不快 *kuài bú kuài* 'fast or not', etc.

[x] (auxiliaries may be negated) is true not only for auxiliaries and full verbs, but also for nouns, adjectives and adverbs, such as 不法 *bùfǎ* 'illegal', 不多 *bùduō* 'not many' and 不很好 *bùhěnhǎo* 'not very good'.

[xii] (auxiliaries do not take aspect markers) and [xiii] (*Aux+N) in Li and Thompson's list have been proposed by Chao in [iii] and [iv] respectively, and problems to these criteria have been discussed above.

[xiv] (auxiliaries cannot be modified by intensifiers) proposed by Li and Thompson and [vi] (auxiliaries my be modified by adverbs of degree) proposed by Chao are contradictory. In fact, as has been discussed above, some auxiliaries can be modified by adverbs while some others can not.

[xv] states that auxiliaries cannot be normalized. Li (2003: 128) argues that this criteria can be exemplified by 可 *kě* 'may', 得 *dé* 'can', 当 *dāng* 'should', 应 *yīng* 'should' and 得 *děi* 'have to', etc. However, many other modal verbs are applicable to this construction, e.g. 应该 *yīnggāi* 'should', 应当 *yīngdāng* 'ought to', 可以 *kěyǐ* 'can' and 可能 *kěnéng* 'may'.

[xi] (auxiliaries cannot occur before subject) in fact is problematic, too. Li (1986: 177) points out that the positive-negative question construction 'Aux+*bù*+Aux' or 'Aux+*ma*?' can occur not only between the subjects and verbal phrase of a sentence, but also before the subject as in (15).

(15) 能　不能　我们　　也　去　看看?　(Li 1986: 169)
Néng bù néng wǒmen　yě　qù　kànkan?
can　not can　we　　also go　have a look
'Can we go and have a look, too?'

[xvii] (Aux-not-Aux question construction) is the same with [viii] proposed by Chao. From the above discussion, we can see that some auxiliaries can occur in the Aux-not-Aux question construction, while some others can not.

Contrary to the statement that an auxiliary may occur independently in elliptical sentences like main verbs while adverbs cannot in [xviii], it is totally acceptable for adverbs to occur independently in elliptical sentences:

(16) Qu: 你　一定　来　吗?

Nǐ yídìng lái ma?
you definitely come QU
'Are you definitely coming?'

An: 一定。

Yídìng.
definitely
'Sure.'

The discussion above shows that none of the 'criteria' can really distinguish the so-called auxiliaries from other verbs or adverbs. Li (2003: 129) summarizes the problems from two aspects. First, each criterion is applicable to some forms, while the excluded forms could be the conventionally central ones. Second, some criteria are applicable to verbs, or even adverbs, not for auxiliaries alone. Hu and Fan (1995: 248) draw a pessimistic conclusion, that is, Chinese auxiliaries manifest greater individuality than generality and, therefore, cannot be established as a category. Li (2003: 129-130) takes a more optimistic point of view toward Chinese modal system with reference to the prototype theory (Ungerer & Schmid 1996) and proposes four core criteria for the Chinese modal system:

A. Occurrence with full verbs
B. Negation with 不 bu 'not'
C. Reduplication not allowed
D. Aspect/phase markers not taken

Li states that A is the elementary property. Only when A is met can a lexical item be an auxiliary verb. B is a verblike property. C and D show that auxiliary verbs are not full-fledged verbs. These four properties can establish Chinese auxiliaries as a unique, but fuzzy, sub-class of verbs, although there are some exceptions.

2.3.3   The Semantic Characterisitcs of Chinese Modals

This section aims to describe the semantic characteristics of

Chinese modals in the order of dynamic modals uses, deontic modals uses and epistemic modals uses.

From Table 2-1, we can see that most modal forms are polysemous. Modals 要 *yào* 'want, must', 能 *néng* 'can' and 得 *děi* 'have to, must' have all the three modal meanings: dynamic, deontic and epistemic. Modals 会 *huì* 'know how to', 用 *yòng* 'need to', 可以 *kěyǐ* 'able to, may' and 该 *gāi* 'should' each have two modal meanings. The remaining four modals 想 *xiǎng* 'desire', 敢 *gǎn* 'dare', 愿意 *yuàn yì* 'willing' and 喜欢 *xǐ huan* 'like' only have dynamic modal meaning.

Table 2-1 Semantic categories of Chinese modals

Modal forms	DY	DE	EP
想 *xiǎng*	●	×	×
会 *huì*	●	×	●
要 *yào*	●	●	●
敢 *gǎn*	●	×	×
用 *yòng*	●	●	×
愿意 *yuànyì*	●	×	×
能 *néng*	●	●	●
可以 *kěyǐ*	●	●	×
该 *gāi*	×	●	●
得 *děi*	●	●	●
喜欢 *xǐhuan*	●	×	×

Notes: ● represents existence of the category. × represents non-existence of the category. DY represents dynamic modals; DE represents deontic modals; EP represents epistemic modals.

1. Dynamic Modal Uses

As can be seen from Table 2-1, all the target modal forms, except 该 *gāi* 'should', have dynamic modal meaning. The remaining ten modals can be roughly divided into three groups: 想 *xiǎng* 'desire', 要 *yào* 'want', 喜欢 *xǐhuan* 'like', 愿意 *yuànyì* 'willing' and 敢 *gǎn* 'dare' expressing notions of desire and intention; 会 *huì* 'know how to', 能 *néng* 'can' and 可以 *kěyǐ* 'able to' expressing the notion of ability; 用 *yòng* 'need to' and 得 *děi* 'have to' expressing the notion of need. Similarities and differences existing among the above dynamic modals are discussed in the following part.

想 *xiǎng* 'desire', 要 *yào* 'want', 喜欢 *xǐhuan* 'like', 愿意 *yuànyì* 'willing' & 敢 *gǎn* 'dare'

想 *xiǎng* 'desire'

As a modal, 想 *xiǎng* 'desire' can only express the dynamic notion of desire, as exemplified by (17).

(17) 我　想　　　到　杭州　　　去　一　趟。
Wǒ xiǎng　dào hángzhōu　qù　yī　tàng.
I　desire　to　Hangzhou　go　one CL
'I want to go to Hangzhou.'
(*A Modern Chinese Dictionary* 1998: 1376)

要 *yào* 'want'

Lü et al (1980: 520) notes that 要 *yào* 'want' expresses 'the will to do something', as in (18).

(18) 我　不　在　你们　　这儿　上学　　　了, 我　要　回去!
Wǒ bú　zài nǐmen　zhè'er　shàngxué　le, wǒ yào　huíqù!
I　not p　your　here go to school PHA　I want to go back
'I don't want to school here, and I want to go back!'
(*Rotation* 转毕淑敏)

Guo (1994: 157) states that 要 *yào* 'want' expresses a stronger desire than 想 *xiǎng* 'desire'. Thus, in requests, 想 *xiǎng* 'desire' is preferred to 要 *yào* 'want' as being more polite.

喜欢 *xǐhuan* 'like'

According to Chao (1968: 734) and Guo (1994: 210), 喜欢 *xǐhuan* 'like' refers to a strong personal preference for certain things or actions, as in (19).

(19) 我　特别　　喜欢　看　　小说。

Wǒ tèbié   xǐhuān   kàn   xiǎoshuō.
I   particularly like   read novel
'I'm extremely fond of reading novels.'

愿意 *yuànyì* 'willing'

愿意 *yuànyì* expresses 'willingness to do something'. In Guo's (1994: 217) opinion, 愿意 *yuànyì* 'willing' can be used interchangeably with 要 *yào* 'want', 想 *xiǎng* 'desire', and 喜欢 *xǐ huan* 'like' in many contexts, but it has quite different meanings. The other three modals represent an active force on the part of the actor to actualize an action or event against some possible resistance, while 愿意 *yuànyì* 'willing' represents a passive resistance on the part of the actor to an external force either explicitly or implicitly imposed on the actor (ibid: 217), as in (20) and (21):

(20) 我 要/想/喜欢   不 工作   就 挣   很 多 钱。
    Wǒ yào/xiǎng/xǐhuān bù gōngzuò jiù zhèng hěn duō qián.
    I want/desire/like   not work then make very much money
    'I want/would like to/like to earn a lot of money without
    having to work '
    (Guo 1994: 217)

(21) 为 了 上   大学, 我 愿意 每 天   晚上   工作。
    Wèi le shàng dàxué, wǒ yuànyì měi tiān   wǎnshàng gōngzuò.
    for go-to college, I willing every day night   work
    'In order to go to college, I'm willing to work every night.'
    (Guo 1994: 217)

敢 *gǎn* 'dare'

Lü (1980: 186) states that 敢 *gǎn* expresses 'someone has the courage to do something', as illustrated by (22).

(22) 你 敢 进来, 算 你   有 胆子!
    Nǐ gǎn jìnlái, suàn nǐ   yǒu dǎnzi!

you dare come in   consider you have guts
'If you dare to come in, you do have guts! '
(*The Yellow Storm* 老舍, 《四世同堂》)

会 *huì* 'know how to', 能 *néng* 'can' & 可以 *kěyǐ* 'able to'

会 *huì* 'know how to'

Wang (1943 [rpt 1985: 70]) points out that 会 *huì* 'know how to' indicates 'acquired capacity'. Zhu (1982: 62) argues that 会 *huì* 'know how to' indicates 'skills acquired by learning or training', as illustrated by (23):

(23) 又 会 吹 笛子, 又   会 拉 手风琴。(Zhu 1982: 62)
Yòu huì chuī dízi, yòu   huì lā shǒufēngqín.
CONJ can blow flute CONJ can play accordion
'(He) can play flute and accordion as well.'

能 *néng* 'can'

In Mandarin Chinese, the basic marker of ability is 能 *néng* 'can'. Lü (1942 [rpt 1982: 246-254]) explicitly states that 能 *néng* 'can' expresses 'whether somebody is capable enough of doing something or not'. Many other linguists, such as Wang (1943 [rpt 1985: 68]), Chao (1968: 735), Tsang (1981: 37), etc., hold similar views on the ability interpretation of 能 *néng* 'can'.

能 *néng* 'can' can be used with an animate subject, expressing the internal ability, as exemplified by (1). It can be used with inanimate subject, indicating a use, a function or a property (Lü 1985: 368), as exemplified by (24):

(24) 他 能 写 会算,   满   可以 当   会计。
Tā néng xiě huì suàn, mǎn   kěyǐ dāng kuàijì.
he can write can calculate completely can work as accountant
'He can write and count, so he can be a very good accountant.'

(Fan, Du & Chen 1987: 101)

(25) 大蒜　　　能　　　　杀　菌。(Lü 1985: 368)
　　　Dàsuàn　néng　　shā　jūn.
　　　garlic　　can　　　kill　virus
　　　'Garlic can disinfect.'

Lü et al (1980: 369) point out that although both 能 *néng* 'can' and 会 *huì* 'know how to' apply to the cases where one has just learned how to perform an action or skill, 会 *huì* 'know how to' is more common, as in (26a). In the cases where one restores one's ability, the only suitable choice is 能 *néng* 'can', as in (26b). We can use both 能 *néng* 'can' and 会 *huì* 'know how to' to express 'have a kind of ability', as illustrated by the first clause in (26c), whereas to indicate reaching a kind of efficiency, we can only use 能 *néng* 'can', as illustrated by the second clause of (26c).

(26) a. 以前　他不会　游泳，　　经过　　练习，现在　会（能）
　　　　Yǐqián tā bú huì yóuyǒng, jīngguò liànxí, xiànzài huì (néng)
　　　　before he not can swim through practice now can (can)
　　　　游 了。
　　　　yóu le.
　　　　swim PHA
　　　　'He couldn't swim before. But now he can after some practice.'
　　　　(Lü et al 1980: 369)

　　b. 我　　病　　好 了，　　能 （*会）劳动　　了。(ibid)
　　　　*Wǒ　bìng　hǎo le,　　néng (*huì) láodòng　le.*
　　　　I　　illness　fine PHA　can (can)　work　　PHA
　　　　'I have recovered and can go back to work.'

　　c. 小李　能 （会）刻 钢板，　一 小时　能 （*会）刻
　　　　*Xiǎolǐ néng(huì) kè　gāngbǎn, yī　xiǎoshí néng (*huì) kè*
　　　　Little Li can (can) cut steel plate.　one hour can (can) cut

一   千   多   字。
yī qiān   duō   zì.
one thousand over word
'Xiao Li can cut stencils. He can cut one thousand words or more an hour.'
(ibid)

可以 *kěyǐ* 'able to'

Gao (1948 [rpt 1986: 237-239]) states that 可以 *kěyǐ* 'able to' indicates 'the ability to perform an action or process' in spoken Chinese as in (27). Li (2003: 157) points out 可以 *kěyǐ* 'able to' can express capacity, use, function, or quality when preceded by an inanimate subject as in (28).

(27) 我 完全   可以   养活   你   嘛。
     Wǒ wánquán   kěyǐ   yǎnghuo nǐ   ma.
     I   totally   can   support you   P
     'I can totally support you.'
     (*A Native of Beijing in New York* 曹桂林《北京人在纽约》)

(28) 星星   之   火, 可以   燎   原。
     Xīngxīng zhī huǒ, kěyǐ   liáo yuán.
     sparks   P fire can   fire prairie
     'A single spark can start a prairie fire.'
     (*Modern Chinese-English Dictionary* 1988: 506)

Lü et al (1980: 369) argue that both 能 *néng* 'can' and 可以 *kěyǐ* 'able to' indicate ability, but 能 *néng* 'can' can be used to express 'good at doing something', but 可以 *kěyǐ* 'able to' can not, as illustrated by (29).

(29) 他 很 能（*可以）吃, 一顿   能（可以）吃四大碗饭。
     *Tā hěn néng (*kěyǐ) chī, yī dùn néng (kěyǐ) chī sì dà wǎn fàn.*
     he very can (can) eat one meal can (can) eat four big bowl rice

'He's a good eater. He can eat four big bowls of rice a meal.'
(Lü et al 1980: 369)

用 *yòng* 'need to' & 得 *děi* 'have to'

用 *yòng* 'need to' expresses the notion of need, and always occurs in its negative form 不用 *bú yòng* 'not need to', as in (30).

(30) 天　　还　　很　　亮,　　不　　用　　开　　灯。
　　　Tiān　hái　hěn　liàng　bú　yòng　kāi　　dēng.
　　　light EMP very bright not need turn on light
　　　'It's still very bright, and there is no need to turn on the light.'
　　　(A *Modern Chinese Dictionary* 1998: 1518)

Lu (1991: 29) states that 得 *děi* 'have to' can indicate 需要 *xūyào* 'need', and exemplifies his interpretation with the examples in (31).

(31) 他身体　很　虚弱, 得　　卧 床　　　休息至 下　星期一。
　　　Tā shēntǐ hěn　xūruò, děi　wò chuáng　xiūxi zhì xià　xīngqīyī.
　　　he body very weak need lie bed rest until next Monday
　　　'He's physically very weak and needs to stay in bed until next Monday.'
　　　(Lu 1991: 29)

In Guo's (1994: 31) opinion, dynamic modal 得 *děi* 'have to' is used when there are personal physical needs that are beyond the individual's volitional control, like hunger, thirst, exhaustion, excretion. The typical use of this word is to refer to the need to go to the bathroom, to drink or eat, or to rest. 得 *děi* 'have to' does not have a negative form *不得 *bù děi* 'not have to'. Therefore, 不用 *bú yòng* 'not need to' is a suppletive negative form for 得 *děi* 'have to'.

2. Deontic Modal Uses

As can be seen from Table 2-1, modal forms 要 *yào* 'must', 用

yòng 'need to', 能 *néng* 'can', 可以 *kěyǐ* 'may', 该 *gāi* 'should' and 得 *děi* 'have to' have deontic modal meaning. The six modals can be roughly divided into three groups: 要 *yào* 'must', 该 *gāi* 'should' and 得 *děi* 'have to' expressing the notion of obligation; 能 *néng* 'can' and 可以 *kěyǐ* 'may' expressing the notion of permission; 用 *yòng* 'need to' expressing the notion of need. Similarities and differences among the above deontic modals are discussed in the following part.

要 *yào* 'must', 该 *gāi* 'should' & 得 *děi* 'have to'

要 *yào* 'must'

要 *yào* 'must' can be used deontically to express obligation or circumstantial need, as in (32a) and (32b) respectively:

(32) a. 读书要 专心;　不 要 　驰鹜。(Li 1924 [rpt 1992: 104])
　　　Dú shū yào zhuānxīn; bú yào chíwù.
　　　read book must attentive; not must careless
　　　'You must concentrate on your study. Don't be careless.'

　　b. 杀人 者　　要　　判　　　死刑。(Tsang 1981: 89)
　　　Shārén zhě yào pàn sǐxíng.
　　　murder PRON must sentence death
　　　'Murderers must be sentenced to death.'

该 *gāi* 'should'

Wang interprets 该 *gāi* 'should' as 'action which should be performed out of morality' (Wang 1943 [rpt 1985: 72]). Ding, Lü, Li, et al (1953 [rpt 1961: 93]), Zhu (1982: 64), Liu, Pan and Gu (1983: 112) provide basically the same explanations: 该 *gāi* 'should' expresses 'need out of reasons, customs, or facts', as in (33):

(33) 男的 该 打 女的,　公公　　　该　　管教　　儿媳妇, 小姑
　　　Nánde gāi dǎ nǔde, gōnggong gāi guǎnjiào ér xífù, xiǎogū
　　　male should beat female, father-in-law should teach son wife, husband's sister

该 给 嫂子 气受, 他们 这 群 男女 信 这个。

gāi gěi sǎozi qìshòu, tāmen zhè qún nánnǚ xìn zhège.

should make sister-in-law angry, they this group man women believe this

(*Lius' Yard* 老舍《柳家大院》)

'Men should hit women, fathers-in-law should discipline their son's wives, husbands' sister should ill treat their brother's wives, that is what these people believe.'

Tsang (1981: 92) and Alleton (1994: 14) make a nice comparison between the obligation modals 该 *gāi* 'should' and 要 *yào* 'must'. With 要 *yào* 'must', especially in cases of directives, the deontic source is largely speaker based. Speaker's involvement is implied. The meaning of 该 *gāi* 'should' is related to a more objective ground, which can be a moral code, a legal norm, or a social convention, as exemplified by (34a). Due to this difference, in some contexts, 要 *yào* 'must' and 该 *gāi* 'should' cannot be substituted for each other, as exemplified by (34b), a sentence uttered by a policeman to a robber who had just removed with force some jewelry from a store and intends to flee. With the utterance, the policeman made the warning and command with his own authority without resorting to outside reasonings.

(34) a. 你 两 天 没 洗澡, 今天 该 洗 了。(Tsang 1981: 92)

Nǐ liǎng tiān méi xǐzǎo, jīntiān gāi xǐ le.

you two day not bathe today should bathe PHA

'You haven't taken a bath for two days. You should take one today.'

b. 不 要 动! (Tsang 1981: 93)

Bú yào dòng!

not must move

'Freeze!'

得 *děi* 'have to'

In Ji (1986: 72), 得 *děi* 'have to' is described as a modal expressing the speaker's strong hope that the hearer does something, as in (35).

(35) 你　得　　去　看　　医生。 (Lu 1991: 30)
    Nǐ　děi　　qù　kàn　yīshēng.
    you must go　see　doctor
    'You've got to see the doctor'

Ding, Lü, Li, et al (1953 [rpt 1961: 92-93]) contend that 得 *děi* 'have to' and 要 *yào* 'must' have similar uses when they indicate 'factual need' or 'necessity'. Wang (1985: 449) claims that 得 *děi* 'have to' can be replaced by 要 *yào* 'must' in general. However, 得 *děi* 'have to' cannot occur alone in answers, whereas as 要 *yào* 'must' can. Ji (1986: 71) puts forward another point about these two modals: semantically 要 *yào* 'must' is not as 坚定 *jiāndìng* 'firmly' as 得 *děi* 'have to'. Therefore, 要 *yào* 'must' is often preceded with the adverb 一定 *yīdìng* 'certainly' in use. Guo (1994: 64) asserts that 要 *yào* 'must' implies a positive attitude with respect to the speaker's endorsement and desire, whereas 得 *děi* 'have to' implies a neutral or sometimes negative attitude with respect to the speaker's endorsement and desire.

能 *néng* 'can' & 可以 *kěyǐ* 'may'

According to Gao (1948 [rpt 1986: 24]), 能 *néng* 'can' can be used in speech to indicate permission. The permission may come from an animate participant (36a) or from certain circumstance (36b). Tsang (1981: 79) claims that 'the use of deontic 能 *néng* 'can' in the positive sense is typically restricted to speech contexts where a question asking for permission is directed to a person who has the power to grant the permission'.

(36) a. 他　能　　坐　到　这　面　　来。(Tsang 1981: 79)
     Tā　néng　zuò　dào　zhè　miàn　lái.

he　can　sit　to　this　side　come
'He can sit over here.'

b. 雨　停　了,　你们　能　回　去　了。(Ibid)

Yǔ tíng　le,　nǐmen néng huí　qù　le.

rain stop PHA　you　can　back　go　PHA

'The rain has stopped. You can go back now.'

Lü (1980: 302) states that 可以 kěyǐ 'may' can be used to express permission, as exemplified by (37). Besides, 可以 kěyǐ 'may' can mean 'deserve', as is exemplified by (38), while 能 néng 'can' does not have that meaning.

(37) 我　可以 提一 个　问题　吗? (Yip & Rimmington 1997: 87)

Wǒ kěyǐ　tí yī　gè　wèntí　ma?

I　may raise　a　CL question P

'May I ask a question?'

(38) 这个　问题　可以　研究　一　番。(Lü 1980)

Zhège　wèntí kěyǐ　yánjiū　yī　fān.

this　problem may　study　one　CL

'This problem deserves further investigation.'

用 yòng 'need to'

Modal 用 yòng 'need to' is primarily a deontic modal, canceling the obligation or necessity to do something.

Chao (1968: 743) points out in his grammar book that the positive answer to a question containing a modal 用 yòng 'need to' uses either the modal 要 yào 'must' or 得 děi 'have to', as shown in (39):

(39) Que: 用　不　用　写　个　收条?

Yòng　bú　yòng xiě　ge　shōutiáo?

need　not　need write　CL　receipt

'Is there a need to write a receipt?'

Ans: (1) 不　　用。

Bú　yòng.

not　need

'It is not necessary.'

(2) 要。

Yào.

must

'Yes. It's necessary.'

(3) 得　　　写　　一　　张。

Děi　xiě　yī　zhāng.

have to　write　one　CL

'Yes. There has to be one.'

3. Epistemic Modal Uses

As can be seen from Table 2-1, modal forms 会 *huì* 'may', 要 *yào* 'must', 能 *néng* 'can', 该 *gāi* 'should' and 得 *děi* 'must' have epistemic modal meaning. The five modals can be roughly divided into two groups: 会 *huì* 'may' and 能 *néng* 'can' expressing notion of possibility; 要 *yào* 'must', 该 *gāi* 'should' and 得 *děi* 'must' expressing notion of necessity. The similarities and differences among the above epistemic modals are discussed in the following part.

会 *huì* 'may' & 能 *néng* 'can'

会 *huì* 'may'

Lü (1942 [rpt 1982: 250]) states that 会 *huì* 'may' can be used to indicate 或然性 *huòránxìng* 'possibility' of an event; concerning with estimation as whether a proposition is true or not. Lu (1991: 246) paraphrases 或然性 *huòránxìng* as 最客观的可能 *zuì kèguānde kěnéng* 'most objective possibility' which indicates that personal assessment of a situation may stem from a relatively objective ground (40a). But Tsang (1981: 66-67) finds that epistemic 会 *huì* 'may' can also be characterized as subjective, as is shown in (40b). He paraphrases 会

huì 'may' as 'likely' or 'more than possible.'

(40) a. 看　　样子　　　会　　下雨。(Zhu 1982: 63)
　　　　Kàn　yàngzi　　huì　xiàyǔ.
　　　　look at appearance may rain
　　　　'It looks as if it's going to rain.'

　　 b. 他　会　　再　　　来　　　的。(Wang 1943 [rpt 1985: 71])
　　　　Tā　huì　zài　　lái　　de.
　　　　he may again come P
　　　　'He may come again.'

According to Li (2003: 140), 会 *huì* 'may' is commonly used in questions, particularly in counter-interrogatives, a kind of forceful statement which has the form of a question, but suggests an answer semantically opposite to the question, as is exemplified by (41).

(41) 你　别　着急　呀,难道　那么　大　个　人　会　丢　了?
　　 Nǐ　bié　zháojí ya, nándào nàme dà　ge　rén　huì　diū le?
　　 you needn't worry P how so　big CL　man　can lose PHA
　　 (Er Nü Yingxiong Zhuan 儿女英雄传 35, from Lü 1942 [rpt 1982: 250])
　　 'Don't worry. He's a big man. How could he be lost?'

能 *néng* 'can'

In the Modern Chinese Dictionary (1998: 921), it is stated that 能 *néng* 'can' indicates possibility in the interrogative sentences, as in (42a). Like 会 *huì* 'may', 能 *néng* 'can' is commonly used in the counter-interrogative, as in (42b).

(42) a. 这　雨　能　下　长　吗?
　　　　Zhè　yǔ　néng　xià　cháng　ma?
　　　　this rain can fall long　P
　　　　'Could the rain last long?'
　　　　(Modern Chinese Dictionary 1996: 921)

b. 他　又　不　是 小 孩子，　又　　是 本地人，　哪　能
   Tā　yòu　bú　shì xiǎo háizi,　yòu　shì běndì rén,　nǎ néng
   he CONJ not be little child CONJ be local person how can

说 丢　　就　丢　了　呢? (Bingxin Wenji 冰心文集 3)
shuō diū　jiù　diū　le　ne?
say lose　EMP lose　PHA P

'He's local and an adult. How could he be lost suddenly?'

Li (2003: 141) asserts that 能 *néng* 'can' can express epistemic possibility in the positive assertion although it is often accompanied by a modal adverb, e.g. 大概 *dàgài* 'possibly', as illustrated by (43).

(43) 早晨　　有　雾, 今天　大概　能　放晴　了。(Lü 1980: 369)
   Zǎochén yǒu　wù, jīntiān dàgài néng fàngqíng le.
   morning there be fog today possibly can be fine P
   'It's foggy early in the morning. Perhaps, we may have a fine day today.'

With epistemic possibility, 能 *néng* 'can' can be used to replace 会 *huì* 'may' in Mandarin Chinese and in most dialects of North China. In other dialects, 会 *huì* 'may' is often preferred to 能 *néng* 'can' (Lü et al 1980: 369; Wang 1985: 443-444). Li (2003: 142) states that 能 *néng* 'can' is less sure about the truth of the proposition compared with 会 *huì* 'may'.

要 *yào* 'must', 该 *gāi* 'should' & 得 *děi* 'must'

要 *yào* 'must'

The CED (A Chinese-English Dictionary 1980: 804) describes that 要 *yào* 'must' can be used to express estimation in sentences of comparison. Alleton (1994: 12-13) states that the most typical use of epistemic 要 *yào* 'must' is with adjectives—she calls them 'quality verbs'. She adds that other modal verbs are also acceptable in this case, but 要 *yào* 'must' gives a nuance of personal appreciation and is considered as 'the best choice', which is illustrated by (44).

(44) 你们　　要　比　　我们　　辛苦　得　多。(CED 1980: 804)
Nǐmen　yào　bǐ　wǒmen　xīnkǔ　de　duō.
you　must than　we　laborious P more
'You must have had a much tougher time than we did.'

Li (2003: 149) disagrees with Alleton's point of view, and asserts that epistemic 要 yào 'must' is not restricted to the sentences of comparison or to quality verbs, as in (45).

(45) 这样,　生活　　水平　　就 要 下 降。(Hu & Fan 1995: 250)
Zhèyàng shēnghuó shuǐpíng jiù yào xià jiàng.
thus　living　standard EMP must down fall
'Thus, the living standard must be going down.'

Lü (1980: 521) asserts that 要 yào 'must' expresses epistemic necessity, which is more sure about the truth of the proposition than that of 可能 kěnéng 'can'. The epistemic necessity indicated by 要 yào 'must' is even near to certainty.

该 gāi 'should'

The epistemic judgment expressed by 该 gāi 'should' indicates what should be the case, but the speaker is not sure. Tsang (1981: 69) states that 该 gāi 'should' carries a certain objective flavor not found in any other modals. That is to say, with this modal the speaker's assessment of the probability about a proposition is based on a relatively objective condition or situation, as in (46):

(46) 下个　月　　她　该　　　回来　　了。(Tsang 1981: 69)
Xiàge　yuè　tā　gāi　huílai　le.
next　month she　should　return　PHA
'She should be returning next month.'

得 děi 'must'

Lü (1980: 143) interpretes 得 děi 'must' as 会 huì 'may'; necessarily like this based on estimation. Lu (1991: 32) asserts that 得 *děi* 'must' is like 会 *huì* 'may', but it is much stronger than 会 *huì* 'may' and more often occurs in speech. Besides, 得 *děi* 'must' is not found in any interrogative sentence.

(47) 这么 晚 才 回去, 妈 又 得 说 你 了。(Lü 1980: 143)
　　 Zhème wǎn cái huíqù, mā yòu děi shuō nǐ le.
　　 this late EMP go back mom again must scold you PHA
　　 'You come back so late. Mom must scold you again.'

2.3.4　The Pragmatic Characteristics of Chinese Modals

Linguists have long observed that the use of modals is context-dependent. The importance of discourse constraints on modals (or any other linguistic items) lies in the simple fact that a word manifests its form and meaning in the discourse. For instance, 能 *néng* 'can' can express dynamic, deontic or epistemic modal notions semantically, but the semantically encoded meanings of 能 *néng* 'can' need to be put in specific discourses to produce the range of readings in (48).

(48) a. 蜜蜂 能 酿 蜜。(Modern Chinese Dictionary 1998: 921)
　　　 Mìfēng néng niàng mì.
　　　 bee　can make　honey
　　　 'Bees can make honey.'

　 b. 你 不 能 不 来 啊。(ibid: 921)
　　　 Nǐ bù néng bù lái a.
　　　 you not can　not come EMP
　　　 'You have got to come.'

　 c. 这 雨 能 下 长 吗? (ibid: 921)
　　　 Zhè yǔ néng xià cháng ma?
　　　 this rain can rain long P
　　　 'Can the rain last long?'

Some Chinese modals allow pragmatic uses like request, suggestion, dissatisfaction, etc. Modal 能 *néng* 'can' can be used in interrogative sentences to request an action (49). It may look like a question about an ability to do something, but it is almost always interpreted as a request to do so. Modal 可以 *kěyǐ* 'may' can be used to make an indirect suggestion (50). It may look like a permission to do something, but in fact it is interpreted as a suggestion. Modals 能 *néng* 'can' and 可以 *kěyǐ* 'able to' can occur in the rhetorical question introduced by the adverb 难道 *nándào* 'how' to express dissatisfaction (51).

(49) 你   能   不 能   说   得   详细   一些? (Li 2003: 286)
     Nǐ   néng bù néng shuō de   xiángxì   yīxiē?
     you can   not can tell P   in detail a bit
     'Can you tell me some details?'

(50) 你   可以   拿去   仔细   读   几   遍。(Li 2003: 288)
     Nǐ   kěyǐ   náqù   zǐxì   dú   jǐ   biàn.
     you may   take away   carefully read a   few time
     'You can take it home and read it times over carefully.'

(51) 难道   你   就   不 能/可以   文明   一点吗? (Li 2003: 288)
     Nándào nǐ   jiù   bù néng/kěyǐ wénmíng yī diǎn ma?
     how   you EMP not can/can civilize a bit P
     'Can't you be a bit more civilized?'

The choice of modals is related to register. Some modals are observable especially in formal writing, while some are observable especially in speech. Take 可/可以 *kě/kěyǐ* 'can' for instance. Ding, Lü, Li, et al. (1953 [1961: 90]) argue that modern spoken Chinese does not use 可 *kě* 'can' alone, but 可以 *kǐyǐ* 'can', except in idiomatic expressions like 可爱 *kě'aì* 'lovable', 可怜 *kělián* 'pitiable', 可靠 *kěkào* 'dependable', 可怕 *kěpà* 'terrible', where 可 *kě* means 'worth' and is closely combined with the subsequent word, being lexicalized into a fixed expression. Li (2003: 156) basically agree with these descriptions proposed by Ding, but would like to argue that 可 *kě* 'can' can also be used in modern Chinese, and the difference between 可 *kě* 'can' and

可以 *kěyǐ* 'can' lies in style. 可 *kě* 'can' occurs more frequently in writings or formal contexts, but 可以 *kěyǐ* 'can' is more popular in speech. Examples 52 and 53 exemplify the differences between 可 *kě* 'can' and 可以 *kěyǐ* 'can' as dynamic modals and deontic modals respectively.

(52) a. 此 厅堂   可   坐   五   百   人。(Li 2003: 156)
       Cǐ tīngtáng   *kě*   *zuò*   *wǔ*   *bǎi*   *rén.*
       this hall   can   sit   five   hundred   people
       'The hall has a seating capacity of 500.'

     b. 可以挑   二   百   斤   的   担子   上   山。(Zhu 1982: 62)
       kěyǐ tiāo   *èr*   *bǎi jīn*   *de*   *dànzi*   *shàng*   *shān.*
       can shoulder two hundred jin P load go up hill
       '(He) can shoulder a load of 100 kg and go up the hill.'

(53) a. 我   也 是 可 去 可 不 去, 本   没有   说定。
       Wǒ yě shì kě qù kě bú qù, běn méiyǒu shuōdìng.
       I   also be may go may not go originally not decide
       (Lü 1942 [rpt 1982: 247]
       'It's not decided yet whether I'll go there or not.'

     b. 我   可以   看看   你的   驾驶   执照   吗?
       Wǒ kěyǐ   *kànkan*   *nǐde*   *jiàshǐ*   *zhízhào*   *ma?*
       I   can   look at   your   drive   license   P
       (Yip & Rimmington 1997: 87)
       'May I have a look at your driving license?'

2.4 The Acquisition of Modality

In view of the importance of the modal system, if children are to become competent members of the target language community, it is crucial for them to have a good mastery of it. Nevertheless, modality turns out to present great challenges for children to acquire, which may partly due to their internal complexity as briefly mentioned in the preceding section. The acquisition of modality usually starts at about 2 years old when children have already acquired hundreds of nouns and verbs, while children of 12 years old or even older come to fully acquire the adult modal system, especially as far as the epistemic uses of modality are concerned. Literature on the development of English modal auxiliaries in child language is quite rich. However, studies on the acquisition of Chinese modal auxiliaries have been scarce. In this section, we first review studies on the acquisition of modality in English and other languages and then studies on the acquisition of Chinese modality.

2.4.1 Previous Studies of Modal Acquisition in English and Other Languages

In this section, we first consider studies that have described children's modal productions in naturally occurring conversations, usually at home, over a period of time. We then examine the data on children's performance in a variety of experimental studies, some of which include children up to middle childhood.

1. Naturalistic Longitudinal Studies

Naturalistic longitudinal studies usually either focus on the semantic aspects or syntactic aspects of modal acquisition. We will first review studies on the semantic aspects, and then studies on the syntactic aspects.

1) Studies on the Semantic Aspects of Modality

A number of studies focusing on semantic aspects of modality (Wells 1979, 1985; Shepherd 1982, 1993; Stephany 1986; Shatz & Wilcox 1991; Bassano 1996; Papafragou 1998; O'Neill & Atance 2000, etc.) all point to the following general conclusion: children start acquiring dynamic and deontic modality before epistemic modality.

Shatz and Wilcox (1991) noted that children learning English acquire modal verbs gradually between 1; 10 (1 year and 10 months) and 2; 6 (2 years and 6 months). Children used *can* or *will* to express ability, intentions and desires as early as 2; 0, and they also used *can't* to express inability in limited syntactic environments, i.e., mainly in declaratives.

Wells (1979) sampled 60 children along with their mothers every three months, from 1; 3 to 3; 6, and then in 1985, he did experiments on a second sample of children followed from age 3; 3 to 5; 0. He finds that children begin expressing dynamic and deontic modality before epistemic modality. The first type of modality that children (at least 50% of the children in the sample) acquired was the expression of ability/inability (using *can/can't*) at 2; 3, which was followed by expression of intention (using *will*) at 2; 6. An average child produced several types of modality by 3; 3, such as ability, permission, willingness/intention, obligation, and necessity. Epistemic modality started slowly from 3; 3 (using *may* and *might*), and these modals were not firmly established until about 5; 0.

Stephany (1986) reviewed modal development in various languages, with foci on Modern Greek and English. In 1993, She reviewed the developmental patterns of modality in German and English. In both investigations, she draws the same conclusion, namely that dynamic and deontic modals are acquired before epistemic ones by children acquiring different languages. For example, English-speaking children expressed intentions and desires with modal auxiliaries such as *can* or *will* and quasi-modals such as *going to/gonna* or *want to/wanna* as early as 2; 0. In contrast, the first epistemically modalized statements (with *may* or *must*) were found to occur in the second half of the third year, about six months later than deontic meanings, and epistemically modalized utterances were extremely rare until the middle of the fourth year. According to Stephany (1993), one reason for this is that children start out predominantly with non-epistemic acts: i.e., requestive or imperative acts, in social interaction. These acts relate to dynamic and deontic modals. Epistemic acts (i.e., declarative acts) are developed later, and hence have later development in epistemic modality.

Languages that have a morphosyntactic system similar to English have shown the same developmental pattern. Smoczyńska (1993) studied the acquisition of Polish modal verbs of four children from 1; 6 to 3; 0 based on diary data. She finds that children used various modal verbs (*móc* [may], *musiec* [must], *wolno* [it is allowed], *trzeba* [there is need], *powinien* [should], *da siq* [(root) possibility]) in dynamic and deontic senses, but not in epistemic senses.

This developmental progression from dynamic and deontic modality to epistemic modality is consistent with the frequency data of the early periods in language development (Wells 1979; Bassano 1996; Torr 1998). In English, Wells (1979) reports a high frequency for the dynamic modals *can* and *will* which express ability and intention respectively, while a relatively low frequency for the epistemic modal *might* which expresses possibility. Bassano (1996) studied the acquisition of epistemic modals by a French child from 1; 9 to 4; 0, and reports that dynamic modals were the most frequent type (44%), followed by deontic ones (39%), while epistemic modals represented 17% of all modals. Torr (1998) investigated the development of modality by an English-speaking child from 2; 6 till 4; 2, and notes that from the beginning of the study expressions of dynamic and deontic modality were consistently more frequent than those of epistemic modality in the child's speech.

The above reviewed studies all converge on the findings that dynamic and deontic modals emerge earlier than epistemic modals. Modals first emerge around 2; 0, while epistemic modals emerge around 2; 6. However, there are a number of studies which show that certain forms and functions of epistemic modality could be acquired earlier.

Bowerman (1986) searched through the semantic, cognitive and pragmatic prerequisites for conditionals to emerge based on the diary notes of three children Christy, Eva and Damon from the time of their first words. She (ibid: 290-291) notes that children around two are capable of conceiving situations that diverge from reality and can express uncertainty about the occurrence of a situation explicitly. Children can express uncertainty about past, present and future situations with rising intonation in languages that use this device for asking questions. For example, when Christy saw her father entering with a pack of photos, she uttered *Daddy buy pictures?* (1; 11). By age 2, or soon after, Christy, Eva and Damon started to indicate uncertainty with additional markers of non-factivity like *maybe, probably, might, could, I think* and *I guess*. For example: *Missy inside maybe?* (Christy 1; 11. C outdoors; friend has vanished); *I don't know. Probably in bed.* (Eva 1; 11. Father hiding under the covers; mother has asked where he is); *I think daddy could do it.* (Christy 2; 2. C struggling with project); *I too big to climb on my plate. I might fall and cry* (Damon 2; 3. In response to mother: Okay, would you like to climb on your plate-your seat?). Bowerman's data accord well with Bate's (1976) observation that children could entertain situations divergent from reality during their second year. They engaged in behaviors showing they knew how to 'suspend truth', for example, pretending to go to sleep. Sometimes they also marked the nontruth of their behavior with a remark like 'No no'. Stephany (1986) also notes that epistemic main verbs like *think* and adverbs like *maybe* may precede epistemically modalized statements.

O'Neill and Atance (2000) examined the use of epistemic modal terms *maybe, possibly, probably* and *might* among 10 children in the CHILDES database between ages 2; 0 and 4; 11, which shows that children of 2; 0 years old are capable of expressing uncertainty with some modal terms. Since none of these children used *possibly*, the uses of the remaining three modal terms were investigated. They discover that children started to use *maybe* and *probably* between 2; 0 and 2; 5, and all three modal terms were productively used from 2; 6. Based on these data, O'Neill and Atance (ibid: 47) propose that "from the results of our study we would suggest that it may not be the case that deontic[1] meanings precede epistemic meanings". They put forward the explanation that the use of modals to express epistemic meanings may have been underestimated in previous studies of modal acquisition in English. These studies mainly focused on children's use of modal auxiliaries and semi-modals *wanna, hafta, gonna, gotta* and *needta*, whereas children's use of epistemic modal terms such as *maybe* and *might* which are more likely to emerge early is not investigated. Their findings suggest that some aspects of epistemic modal notions are within the capability of children younger than age three. O'Neill and Atance note future work should define more clearly various meanings of epistemic modality, especially with respect to those first expressed by children as young as age two.

Recent data suggest that particular deeply grammaticalized devices expressing epistemic meanings can be found earlier. Choi (1991) studied the speech of three Korean children and traced the acquisition of four modal suffixes. The suffixes, which belong to an obligatory class of verbal inflections called sentence-ending (SE) suffixes, occur in informal interaction and are used to mark the status of the speaker's knowledge, i.e. evidential[2] relations. To be specific,

---

1 Here 'deontic meanings' is a cover term for dynamic meanings and deontic meanings.

2 These suffixes express the speaker's assessment of the information status (e.g. whether the information is new or old, or shared or not shared with the listener) and source of information (e.g. whether the event/state of affairs is directly or indirectly perceived). These markers are typically termed evidentials. It is debatable whether evidentiality is part of epistemic modality. The problematic relation between evidentiality and epistemic modality is not surprising, since there is a logical connection between them in the sense that epistemic judgments are conceptually based on evidence, and evidentials refer to types of the latter. In line with this, evidential categories often suggest or imply a certain degree of probability of the state of affairs.

the suffix -*ta* indicates new/unassimilated knowledge in the speaker's mind, whereas -*e* marks old/assimilated information. The suffix -*ci* (or a stronger form, -*cyana*) indicates that the information is certain and is shared by both the speaker and the listener. The suffix-*tay* introduces indirect evidence (e.g. hearsay or reported speech). According to Choi, these suffixes were acquired between 1; 9 and 2; 6, roughly in the order mentioned above. The first two (-*ta* and -*e*) were acquired before 2; 0, and the other two between 2; 1 and 2; 6. The data suggest that Korean children acquired these forms by 2; 6, the period when English-learning children are reported to just began acquiring epistemic modals. Choi herself has suggested some possible factors which may facilitate the acquisition of Korean modal SE suffixes: their perceptual salience (given their sentence-final position), their obligatoriness (and thus the richer input they provide to the acquisitional device), and their semantic consistency (they do not communicate root meanings, neither do they incorporate tense or aspectual meanings). Another two studies on the acquisition of Japanese sentence-final particles (Clancy 1985) and Turkish verb suffixes (Asku-Koc 1998) also show that children began acquiring the evidential markers of their languages from early on.

Bassano (1996) investigated the functional and formal constraints on the emergence and early development of epistemic modality based on the longitudinal data of a French child between 1; 9 and 4; 0, which reveals that the epistemic function of prediction and lexicalized epistemic markers may be acquired early. She proposes that epistemic modal functions fall into the following three categories: assertive modalization, disassertive modalization and prediction. Assertative modalizations refer to qualifications which mark the speaker's complete adhesion to the truth of the asserted proposition, whereas disassertative modalizations are characterized by properties of non-factivity or contra-factivity. Predictions are speakers' judgments about the future accomplishment or non- accomplishment of events or processes. Assertive and disassertive modalizations are prototypical functions of epistemic modality. The formal devices marking epistemic modality in French are highly diversified, since French does not possess a true set of modal auxiliaries forming a distinct grammatical class (like English or German) on the basis of a range of syntactic criteria. French epistemic markers include cognitive modal verbs, various lexicalized verbal devices, grammatical markers (conditional mood, future and imperfect tenses) and syntactic particles with modal value.

Bassano's study reveals that the first function to emerge was prediction, found in the first month of the third year. Two other epistemic functions then emerged more or less together during the first half of the third year. Finally, disassertive modalization grew richer during the second half of the third year. The early emergence of prediction can be considered as primers that prepare the appearance of prototypical functions later.

The development of formal markers of epistemic modality brings out two evolutionary processes: a formal complexification process and a grammaticalization process. The complexification process denotes the fact that modal marking evolves from formally simple devices to more complex constructions. The grammaticalization process indicates that the development of epistemic modal markings partially depends on the degree to which the markings are lexicalized vs. grammaticalized. Overall, highly grammaticalized devices, such as grammatical future, conditional mood and conjunctive particle, appear later than lexicalized devices such as adjectives, adverbs and main verbs. Lexicalization thus appears to favour the emergence of epistemic devices in French. Such a lexicalization effect would seem to disagree with Choi's (1991) conclusion that the early appearance of epistemic devices in young Koreans' speech is related to the fact that these devices are deeply gramaticalized into verbal suffixes. Bassano (ibid: 107) asserts that the two results are not contradictory. She proposes a distinction must be made between obligatory grammaticalized markings and non-obligatory grammaticalized markings. Obligatory grammaticalized markings may be used early in some languages such as Korean and Japanese, while non-obligatory grammaticalized markings turn out to be more difficult to construct than lexicalized ones in a language such as French. These evolutionary processes provide examples of how the degree to which markings are lexicalized vs. grammaticalized can influence the development of epistemic modality.

To sum up, the above reviewed cases seem to converge on the point that the onset of epistemic modality follows that of dynamic and deontic modality, and typically appears around or after 2; 6. However, studies also show that epistemic modality could appear earlier in the following situations: English epistemic modal markers *maybe*, *probably*, *might*, *could*, *I think* and *I guess*; Korean, Japanese, or Turkish grammaticalized suffixes expressing evidentiality; or French lexicalized epistemic markers expressing prediction. The earlier emergence of certain forms and functions of epistemic modality shows that some epistemic modal notions are within the grasp of children around 2; 0.

2) *Studies on the Syntactic Aspects of Modality*

Compared with the rich literature on the acquisition of semantics of modals, studies on the syntactic aspect have been scarce, and the findings of these studies have been mixing.

Fletcher (1978) studied the acquisition of verb phrases by a child named Daniel from 2; 0 to 2; 2 by taking diary notes, and discovered that the syntactic structures of modal utterances develope quickly from simple declaratives to questions. In Fletcher's study, twenty instances of modal utterances were recorded. The modal forms that emerged during the two months period were *can't, can, willn't, will* and *shall*, which appeared in declaratives, inverted yes-no questions and tag questions. Declarative was the most frequently occurring sentence type, accounting for 75% of total modal utterances, and questions accounted for the remaining 25%. Modal *can* appeared in all the three kinds of structures: declaratives, inverted yes-no questions and tag questions. To mention a few examples of modal utterances containing *can*: *can't do my zip up, can you do that daddy, can I blow candles out, can I*. Modal *will* appeared in declaratives and inverted yes-no questions. The remaining modal forms *can't, willn't* and *shall* only occurred in declaratives or inverted yes-no questions.

The quick development of syntactic structures revealed by Fletcher's (1978) study is challenged by the findings of Shatz, Billman, and Yaniv (1986), who find that syntactic structures of modal utterances change slowly. Shatz, Billman and Yaniv (1986) examined the modal productions of 30 children bimonthly for a six-month period, beginning when the mean age of the children was 2, 2. These children were selected because they seemed ready to acquire auxiliaries: When first seen, they were regularly producing subject-verb-object utterances but very few auxiliaries. The researchers discover that modal vocabulary develop quickly since 2; 2, but the syntactic structures, in contrast, develop slowly. Shatz et al. analyzed the kinds of constructions in which modal words and concatenatives appeared. Full forms and contractions were considered as separate types. For example, *'ll* and *will* were separate word types, as were *can* and *can't*. Word types were then scored for whether they appeared in yes-no questions, yes-no inverted questions, wh-questions, tag questions, declaratives, or imperatives. Although the children produced on average five different word types, more than 83% of the modal word types appeared only in declaratives. Shatz and Wilcox

(1991: 331) note that "while modal vocabulary growth proceeds fairly rapidly during this period, the range of syntactic constructions in which the modals appear changes somewhat more slowly." In comparison with Fletcher's findings, Shatz et al's study reveals that early modal acquisition is more lexically than syntactically driven. Shatz et al., however, admitted that the bimonthly sampling procedure may have underestimated the productivity of modal forms.

The above two studies addressed the syntactic structures of modal utterances from the aspect of sentence types modals appear, and have come to opposite conclusions. Diessel (cited in Tomasello 2003: 246-248), on the other hand, investigated the development of subjects and verbs of modal utterances.

Diessel investigated four children up to 5 years of age in quantitative detail on their acquisition of complex sentences, and he mentioned the syntactic development of concatenatives *wanna*, *hafta*, and *gotta* while discussing the acquisition of to-infinitives. He found that WANNA, HAFTA, and GOTTA emerged at about 2; 3 and accounted for over 90 percent of all the to-infinitives over the course of the entire study. The children used these concatenatives in very formulaic ways: almost all the subjects were the first-person pronoun I, the verbs were in present tense and were not negated. The constructions involved may be represented by:

I wanna VERB PHRASE
I hafta VERB PHRASE
I gotta VERB PHRASE

From age 2 to age 5, children's growing linguistic sophistication with to-infinitives is manifest in three main ways. First the subjects became less formulaic and more diverse, for example, third-person subjects emerged ('*Dolly wanna drink that*'). Second, children learned a wider range of matrix verbs, for example, *I forgot to buy some soup.*

Third, they learned more complex constructions with an NP between the two verbs.

The syntactic development of modal utterances in Daniel's data (Fletcher 1978), however, did not follow the route from formulaic constructions to diverse constructions as proposed by Diessel. The first modal utterance by Daniel was the bare negative form *can't* when he was suck in a large pot and was unable to get out. The second modal utterance was *you can* as an answer to daddy's question *can daddy go and get his tea*. The third utterance was *can't do my zip up* as an answer to caregiver's question *can't what, Daniel*. Following these first utterances, complex sentence structures emerged quickly, as in *shall I do that, I can come in your bed, will you do that again for me, and so on*. It is clear from the above examples that the syntactic structures of modal utterances in Daniel's speech did not develop from formulaic structures to diverse structures as stated by Diessel. Rather, it seems the modal utterances developed from simple structures to complex structures quickly.

Apart from the above investigations of the syntactic aspects of modal utterances, some other researchers address the relationship between specific type of modality and sentence type, as well as the relationship between specific type of modality and subjecthood.

There seems to be a relation between specific type of modality and sentence type. Pea and Mawby (1984) report that most of the modals (e.g. *gonna, want*) were used in the affirmative. Negative modal values were only used to express constraints on action or an unwillingness to act (e.g. *can't, won't*) at the time of speaking.

There also seems to be a relation between specific type of modality and subjecthood. For example, Pea and Mawby (1984) examined the semantics of modal auxiliary verbs (*can, will, gonna*) in six children aged between 2; 4 and 2; 10. They find that children used dynamic modals with first person pronoun *I* to express volition of the self 80% to 95% of the time (e.g. *I will give you a tiny little fork*).

To sum up, the findings on the syntactic development of modal utterances are mixing. Some researchers assert that the sentence types of early modal utterances are overwhelmingly declaratives, whereas others find diverse sentence types from the beginning of modal acquisition. Some researchers note a developmental progression from formulaic to diverse structures of modal utterances, while others' data show a wide range of syntactic structures in early modal utterances. Researches also show that the semantics of modals is related to their syntactic structures in certain ways.

2. Experimental Studies

Major findings on the developmental pattern of modality come from longitudinal studies of children's spontaneous speech. Experimental studies have mainly examined some detailed aspects of the way children acquire epistemic modal meanings as well as children's ability to distinguish differences among modal meanings.

Hirst and Weil (1982) performed an experiment to examine children's ability to comprehend differences among modal meanings. They asked children to distinguish between sentences containing modals in two tasks, one an object-search paradigm focusing on epistemic meanings and the other a directive-action paradigm focusing on deontic meanings. In their study, Hirst and Weil asked 54 children aged 3 to 6; 6 to distinguish between modals of different strengths. Hirst and Weil find an ordering of ability to distinguish the strength of the terms such that the greater the distinction in strength between the two modal words, the younger the age at which a distinction was reliably made. They found that by 5; 6 all the pairs in the epistemic task were distinguishable, and even the 3-year-olds made some reliable distinctions. On the deontic task, however, only the 6-year-olds made reliable distinctions. This is unexpected, as naturalistic data have shown that deontic meanings are acquired earlier than epistemic meanings. Hirst and Weil (1982) point out that epistemic tasks were pretty straight-forward, whereas the deontic ones were more complex.

Moore, Pure and Furrow (1990) tested children's understanding of a broad range of modal forms: modal verbs, *must*, *might* and *could*, and modal adjuncts, *probably*, *possibly*, and *maybe*, as well as mental verbs, *know* and *think*. The experimenters followed Hirst and Weil's technique by giving contrasting pairs of modal sentences (using puppets) as clues to the location of an object. The results show that 3 years old did not differentiate between any of the modal contrasts presented, whereas 4 years old and older children were able to find the hidden object on the basis of what they heard. Children performed better for the pairs of terms with a maximal contrast between them (e.g. *probably* vs. *maybe*) than for the pairs with a relatively minimal contrast (e.g. *possibly* vs. *maybe*). Moore et al.'s study replicated the findings of Hirst and Weil's experiment, which suggests that the ability does not come from acquisition of particular lexical items but rather from a more general understanding of the mental state concept of relative certainty.

Other studies have shown that a full understanding of epistemic modality takes a few more years. Bassano's experimental studies (Bassano, Hickmann and Champaud 1992; Champaud, Bassano and Hickmann 1993) with French children show that some epistemic modals were not fully understood till eight years of age. Modals expressing the conditions under which certainty is assessed were understood at 4; 0, while those expressing uncertainty were not fully understood till 8; 0.

Coates' study (1988) revealed that metalinguistic analysis of the modal system is achieved at an even later age. Coates conducted a classification task with modal markers in English. She asked adult,

12-year-old and 8-year-old subjects to sort cards, each containing a modalized version of the sentence '*I visit my grandmother tomorrow*' into piles on the basis of similarity of meaning. Cluster analysis revealed four distinct groups in the adult system:

(a) epistemic possibility (may, might, perhaps, possible that, probably);

(b) possibility/ability/permission (can, could, nothing prevents, allowed, able, possible for);

(c) intention/prediction/futurity (will, shall, going to, intend);

(d) obligation/necessity (must, should, ought, have got to, obliged).

Twelve-year-olds' categorization was similar to the adults' with some minor differences. Eight-year-olds did not include a category for epistemic modality, and they were less consistent among themselves in their classification. Coates concludes that the mastery of the modal system is achieved at a relatively later age.

The experimental studies reviewed so far can be summarized as follows. There is a gradual development in the level of abstraction in children's understanding of modality. Children start developing epistemic notions from about 3 years of age, and 4 year olds are much better than 3 year olds in understanding tasks involving epistemic modal markers. It takes a few more years to reach a high level of abstraction that allows children to classify modal terms into semantic categories. The greater the distinction in strength between two modals, the younger the age at which a distinction was reliably made. Naturalistic studies on the acquisition of modality indicate that children begin producing epistemic modals at around 2; 6, which is earlier than the findings of experimental studies. The discrepancy is probably due to a certain degree of unnaturalness inherent in experimental tasks. The artificial tasks presented in experiments are probably more difficult for children to process. Nevertheless, experimental studies are valuable as they complement the findings of longitudinal naturalistic studies by providing insight into the extent to which modal meanings are understood at a given developmental period (Choi 2006).

2.4.2 Previous Studies of Modal Acquisition in Chinese

Literature on the acquisition of Chinese modal auxiliaries is scarce. Until now, there are only two studies available on the acquisition of Chinese modality. Mary Erbaugh (1982) carried out a study focusing on the pragmatic context for the acquisition of Chinese syntax. The study was based on 64 hours of audio-taped longitudinal home visits with four Chinese children aged 1; 10 through 3; 10 in Taibei, Taiwan. All four were Chinese monolinguals, selected after interviews with 20 Chinese-speaking families who had immigrated to Taiwan from north China. Erbaugh audio-taped hour-long visits with Pang, a girl aged 1; 10, and Kang, a boy aged 2; 10, every other week for 12 months from 1979 to 1980. She also recorded 7 hour-long visits with Laohu, a boy aged 2; 0, over 2 weeks' time and 9 hours with a girl, Zhongrong, aged 2; 6, in an 8-week period in 1976.

The acquisition of modals occupies only a tiny part in Erbaugh's research. She reports that children started to use modal auxiliaries 会 *huì* 'can' and 要 *yào* 'want' between 1; 10 to 2; 4, and the two modals remained rare except in answer to adult questions. For Pang, the only auxiliary productive in her spontaneous speech between 1; 10 to 2; 4 was 会 *huì* 'can'. 会 *huì* 'can' in isolation, as an answer to an adult question, came in first; next came the negative form 不会 *bú huì* 'can't', also appearing alone in answer to adult questions. Finally, 会 *huì* and 不会 *búhuì* appeared, more or less simultaneously, with other verbs, as in 这个会跌倒 *zhè ge huì diēdǎo* 'This could fall over' in describing a shaky block tower; or 我会做一个游泳池 *wǒ huì zuò yī ge yóuyǒngchí* 'I can make a swimming pool'. Erbaugh proposes that the quiz style of conversation for Chinese and the lack of a separate word for 'yes' or 'no' might have facilitated modal acquisition in Chinese. During 2; 6-3; 2, most of the full range of available modal auxiliaries appeared in spontaneous declarative speech. These include not only 会 *huì* 'can' which was the only common modal during 1; 10-2; 4, but also 能 *néng* 'able', 可以 *kěyǐ* 'may', as well as 敢 *gǎn* 'dare' and 应该 *yīnggāi* 'must'. The most frequently used form was 要 *yào* 'want' at that time. The pattern of isolated use in answer to a question, appearing before spontaneous use with a complement, held true for the above modals as they emerged for Pang and Kang.

Guo (1994) studied the syntactic forms, semantic meanings, and discourse functions of Chinese modal auxiliaries in children's speech. His research focuses on how modal notions such as desire, ability, need, permission, obligation, circumstantial possibility and necessity, and logical possibility and necessity are employed in children's daily interactive discourse, and how children's communicative goals in interpersonal interaction serve as a structuring frame and motivation force for the development of these modal concepts.

The data were collected from naturalistic discourse in cooperative interactive play by Chinese-speaking children of 3, 5, and 7 years of age living in Beijing. For each age group, six children were selected, three girls and three boys. The six children were organized into two play groups, with one group consisting of two girls and one boy, and the other, two boys and one girl. Each play group was asked to engage in three different sets of semi-structured activities, 1) cooperative lego construction, 2) role play with dolls (guò jiājiā in Chinese, in which the subjects can either take the role themselves or assign roles to the dolls), and 3) making objects with playdough, and collectively solving picture puzzles. Each play group was visited twice a week at school and was asked to engage in one set of activities for one hour in each visit. Each play group was engaged in each set of activities twice, resulting in a total of six one-hour sessions for each group. In total, 12 hours of child interactions were video-recorded for each of the three age groups. The use of eleven Chinese modal auxiliaries were investigated: 会 *huì* 'know how to, may', 能 *néng* 'can', 可以 *kěyǐ* 'able to, may', 想 *xiǎng* 'desire', 要 *yào* 'want, must', 喜欢 *xǐhuan* 'like', 愿意 *yuànyì* 'willing', 敢 *gǎn* 'dare', 该 *gāi* 'should', 得 *děi* 'have to' and 用 *yòng* 'need to'. The following findings were reported: 1) Children's focus on notions of modality changed with age. Three-year-olds focused on notions of personal ability and desires, which may have led to frequent use of dynamic modals. Five-year-olds focused on notions of permission and obligation, which may have led to frequent use of deontic modals. Seven-year-olds started to get interested in logical reasoning, which may have led to frequent use of epistemic modals. 2) Children's early use of modals was deeply rooted in the ongoing interpersonal interaction. The meaning and form of the modal utterances heavily depended on the communicative goals to which these utterances were put. The final product of the sentence form, semantic interpretation, and discourse effect was the result of the actions and interactions of form, meaning and function. 3) Children's interpersonal and communicative goals had a formative motivating power on the form and meaning of the modal auxiliaries and their consequent changes, leading to the development of the modal system. Mechanisms DISCOURSE FOCUS SHIFTING, DISCOURSE BRIDGING and DISCOURSE FRAMING were hypothesized. Through these mechanisms, children's daily interpersonal practices, in which modal auxiliaries were used, directed and redirected children's attention to different aspects of the phenomenon that modals encode.

Compared with the rich literature on modal acquisition in English, studies on Chinese modal acquisition are inadequate in the following aspects: (1) Erbaugh's discovery that children acquired the first modals 会 *huì* 'know how to' and 要 *yào* 'want' in its dynamic sense around 2 years old is in line with the time of emergence of modals in other languages. However, her research only briefly mentioned the modals acquired from 1; 10 to 3; 10. The order of emergence of modal forms, the semantic and syntactic feature of the modals acquired and the factors constraining the acquisition of modals were not discussed at all. (2) Research findings on modal acquisition of different languages seem to converge on the point that the first emergence of modal expressions starts at about age 2, and the onset of epistemic modality follows that of dynamic and deontic modality, which typically appears around 2; 6. Guo studied the modal utterances of 3, 5 and 7 years old children. His study, therefore, can not convey any information about the emergence and early development of Chinese modality. (3) Input studies of modality show that input influences the child's course of acquisition, which is mediated by the processing characteristics and limitations of the child, while none of the above studies in Chinese has discussed the interaction of modal input and children's social-cognitive development during the acquisition process.

2.5   Theoretical Accounts of L1 Modal Acquisition

Studies on modal acquisition seem to show the same acquisitional order: root modality is acquired before epistemic modality. Why is it so? Different explanations have been advanced in the literature to account for L1 acquisition of English modality.

2.5.1   Perkin's Explanation

Taking a Piagetian framework, Perkins (1983) attributes the early development of *can* and *will* in the preoperational stage to the child's egocentrism, which is also invoked to explain the absence of 'abstract' terms *must* and *may*. Since children are 7 years old they enter the concrete operational stage, when the negotiation of social roles and tasks begins. This period coincides with the proliferation of expressions of dynamic and deontic modality. Finally, since children are 11 years old they enter the formal operational stage, when the abstract representation of alternative hypotheses and their deductive implication start to emerge. This period coincides with the productive use of epistemic modality.

The basic problem with Perkins's proposal, according to Papafragou (1998: 378), is that it gets the facts wrong. Findings of naturalistic studies show that the first instances of epistemic modality appear around the third year, which is much earlier than a Piagetian account would allow. Findings of experimental studies suggest that children may entertain and process logical possibilities by 7 years (if not earlier), which is also much earlier than Piaget's estimated threshold for logical reasoning in children. Moreover, findings of studies on the acquisition of mental terms (such as *think, know, guess*) reveal that 3-year-olds can use these mental terms to refer to their own mental contents, which seems not to be tied to a simple, concrete mode of thinking. All in all, young children seem to be capable of handling the concepts of mental representation and related epistemic concepts much earlier than the Piagetian framework credited them with.

2.5.2 The Theory of Mind Hypothesis

Understanding epistemic notions is related to the development of theory of mind in children (Gopnik & Astington 1988; Papafragou 1998, Moore, Pure & Furrow 1990). Theory of mind is the ability to attribute mental states —beliefs, intents, desires, pretending, knowledge, etc. —to onself and others and to understand that others have beliefs, desires and intentions that are different from one's own (Premack & Woodruff 1978).

One of the most important milestones in theory of mind development is gaining the ability to attribute false belief: that is, to recognize that others can have beliefs about the world that are wrong. False belief understanding is usually tested by carrying out three kinds of false-belief tasks (Wimmer & Perner 1983; Gopnik & Astington 1988; Zaitchik 1990; Leslie & Thaiss 1992; etc.). First, a standard change-in-location false-belief task acted out with dolls: A doll leaves an object in one place, and while the doll is away, the object is moved to a new place. Then the doll returns and children are asked where the doll will look for the object. Second, a standard unexpected-contents false-belief task: children are asked what is inside a familiar box, and they answer with the usual contents. Then the box is opened and is found to have unusual contents. After these unexpected contents are replaced in the box, children are asked again what is inside the box, what they thought was inside it before it was opened, and what their friends, who have not seen inside the box, would think inside it before the box was opened. Third, a standard appearance- reality task: children are shown an object that looks like one thing and is really something else (e.g. a sponge painted to look like a rock). They are asked what the object looks like, what it really is, what their friend would think it is when they first see it. These tasks involve the ability to appreciate that people stand in different and variable informational relations to the world—hence beliefs can vary, they may occasionally be false, and they are often modified or updated as new evidence becomes available (Papafragou 1998: 161). Children standardly fail false belief tasks before the age of 4; 0 or 5; 0.

Papafragou (1998: 382-383) constructs an account of the acquisition of modal verbs by elaborating a link between epistemic modality and the child's developing theory of mind. Two-year-olds have a non-representational grasp of desire and perception. Desires refer to drives towards objects; perceptions refer to awareness of visual contact with objects. From this initial understanding of desire and perception as simple causal links between the mind and the world, 3-year-olds go on to develop a non-representational conception of belief. Belief contents are taken to reflect the world directly (the 'copy theory', as Wellman 1990, calls it). Children of 3 years old, therefore, notoriously fail to detect misrepresentation and can not acknowledge that beliefs may have different sources or come with varying degrees of conviction. Children of 4; 0 or 5; 0 years old seem to have developed a 'representational model of mind'. They come to understand that almost all psychological functioning (desires, perceptions, beliefs, pretences, and images) is mediated by representations of reality. Mental representations are increasingly employed to explain human thought and action. Expressions of epistemic modality obviously fit into a representational model of the mind, since epistemic modals like *may, might, must, should, will* and *ought to* indicate that a certain proposition is entailed by/compatible with the speaker's belief-set. The use of epistemic modality depends crucially upon the ability to reflect on the content of one's own beliefs, to take into consideration the reliability of those beliefs, and to perform deductive operations on them.

As has been discussed above, the Theory of mind is essential for the acquisition of epistemic modals, but meanwhile the acquisition of modal expressions actually facilitate the development of theory of mind (Farrar & Maag 2002). Farrar and Maag (2002) examined the relationship between children's language ability at 2; 0 and their theory of mind performance at 4; 0. Language ability was assessed by parental report, by analyzing children's speech in naturalistic play sessions, as well as by testing their verbal memory of sentences of different lengths. Children's level of theory of mind was assessed by their performance on understanding of false belief, representational change, and appearance-reality tasks. Results show there exist a significant interrelation between early language ability and later theory of mind performance. Children had a high vocabulary level at 2; 0 did better in the theory of mind tests at 4; 0. Their study suggests a specific link between early language ability and later theory of mind development.

To sum up, the relationship between modal acquisition and cognition is interactive and bi-directional.

2.5.3   Caregiver Input and Acquisition of Modality

Studies have shown that maternal speech has important bearings on modal form, meaning, and syntax children learn and use frequently at an early stage. Wells' (1979) study confirms the likelihood that the lexical characteristics of input affect the order of acquisition of modals. Wells reports that *will* and *can* were the two modals used by 100% of the 60 mothers in his sample, with *will* occurring in 1869 utterances and *can* in 1201 utterances. These two modals were the earliest ones emerged, as well as the most frequently occurring modals in children's speech. Modal *can* was used by 98% of the 60 children in 1210 utterances, and *will* was used by 100% of the children in 840 utterances. Modal *may*, in contrast, was only used by 13% of the mothers in 18 utterances, and this modal emerged late and was only used by 17% of the children in 25 utterances.

Shatz, Grimm, Wilcox, et al. (1990) conducted a study on modal meanings in maternal speech by comparing the frequency and function of modal verbs in the speech of eight German-speaking mothers with those of modal auxiliaries in the speech of eight U.S. mothers as they talked to their children of mean age 2; 5, and again four months later. Their study discovers that epistemic modals, which English-learning children acquire late, were observed to be quite infrequent in mothers' speech (10% of all modals in mothers' speech to children aged 2; 5). Thus, the developmental pattern of acquiring dynamic and deontic modals earlier than epistemic modals is at least in part related to the frequency of input in mothers' speech. They also coded modal meanings into eight categories of semantic functions, including agreement, intention, permission, obligation, necessity, possibility, conditional, and enablement. For both groups of mothers, intention and possibility were the most frequent meanings conveyed to the children. Almost all the other meanings were at least half as frequent as these two. The children's early modal uses were coded as well, and intention and possibility were found to account for more than two-thirds of the instances of modal use. There were significant correlations between groups of mothers and children on the frequency of modal word types for both languages and a significant correlation on the frequency of semantic categories for German.

Research on syntax, focusing not on modals, but on the whole auxiliary system, has also found effects of maternal auxiliary use on child acquisition. Correlating some aspects of maternal speech at one time of measurement with auxiliary growth in children at a later time, researchers have found some positive relations between maternal speech and frequency of auxiliary use in children. However, this line of research has not produced unequivocal answers to the questions of which specific aspects of the input are efficacious and what the mechanism of facilitation is (Hoff-Ginsberg & Shatz, 1982; Shatz, Hoff-Ginsberg & MacIver, 1989).

However, high frequency does not always explain children's early modal development. Wells (1979) observes that although mothers use some modal forms quite frequently, the frequencies of these modal forms in children's speech are low. For example, *would* was used by 83% of the mothers in 128 utterances, whereas it was only used by 22% of the children in 25 utterances. Modal *ought* was used by 27% of the mothers in 23 utterances, whereas it was only used by 3% of the children in 2 utterances. Shatz and Wilcox (1991) note that children can acquire modals that are relatively rarely used by the mothers. For example, in their study, young German children expressed necessity with modal forms although their mothers used it quite rarely (once or a few times). This suggests that there is more than linguistic input that determines the child's developmental pattern of modality. In Choi's (1991, 1995) studies, he looked at the relation between mothers' input frequency and the order of acquisition of the SE suffixes by their children. He finds only a partial relation between input frequency and acquisition order. Korean mothers used the suffix -e most frequently followed by -ci, -ta, and -tay, in that order. The difference in frequency between -e and -ta was quite large, 35% vs. 8%, respectively, on average in mothers' speech. In their children's speech, however, -ta was first acquired followed by -e. The early acquisition of -ta, despite a low frequency in mothers' speech, can be explained by its salience in semantic and pragmatic properties. It marks new information that is perceptually salient in the here-and-now and is of interest to the child.

In summary, studies on both the syntactic and semantic aspects of modal development strongly suggest that the frequency with which children hear particular forms and meanings affects the course of their acquisition. However, it is also clear that the nature of the input itself cannot fully determine the child's course of acquisition. The influence of the input may need to be mediated by other factors, such as linguistic factors and children's cognitive development.

2.5.4 A Converging Constraints Model

Shatz and Wilcox (1991) propose 'a converging constraints model' to account for the complicated process of modality acquisition. The basic idea is that there are a variety of constraints, such as input, cognitive processing, form-function relational and universal grammatical, that operate on modal acquisition and different constraints apply at different times in children's modal development.

In their model, constraints are "factors that channel or direct the process of acquisition" (Shatz & Wilcox 1991: 340).

Shatz and Wilcox note that progress toward the adult system could be achieved when old constraints no longer operate and new ones are called into play. When children develop cognitively and input broadens, they have the opportunity to notice new meanings for modality that may not have occurred or may have gone unnoticed previously. Similarly, increased attention to syntactic and semantic similarities between modality and other auxiliaries may lead to reorganization of earlier, narrower categories into a more general, abstract one. Over the course of acquisition, the various constraints operating on the system produce a convergence on the adult model.

2.6 Research Questions

For the last two decades, researches on the acquisition of modality in children's language have been trying to find out the pattern in which various modal forms, meanings and syntactic structures are acquired and the underlying mechanisms to explain the patterns. Studies in English and other languages show that children begin to acquire modality before 2 years old, and dynamic and deontic modalities are acquired before epistemic modalities. Some researchers assert that the syntactic structures of modal utterances develop from formulaic constructions to diverse constructions slowly, whereas other researchers assert that the development follows the route from simple constructions to complex constructions relatively quickly. Various factors have been proposed to explain the developmental patterns of modality: linguistic complexity, cognitive development and caregivers' input. There are only two studies available on the acquisition of Chinese modality. Erbaugh's (1982) study is too cursory to discover the developmental process in detail.

While Guo's (1994) cross-sectional study aims at the modal development and use by three groups of children aged 3, 5 and 7 years old, which in nature is not a naturalistic longitudinal study on the acquisition of modality and thus reveals nothing about the ontogenesis of Chinese modality. To fill the gap of Chinese modal acquisition in the literature, the present study will be carried out and aims to answer the following research questions:

1. What is the order of emergence of Chinese modal forms in the child's data and what are the developmental patterns of modal forms in the child's data across time periods?

2. Do dynamic and deontic modals emerge earlier than epistemic modals in the child's data and what are the developmental patterns of the three semantic categories of modals in the child's data across time periods?

3. Do the syntactic structures of modal utterances in the child's data evolve from formulaic structures to diverse structures or from simple structures to complex structures and what are the developmental patterns of the syntactic structures of modal utterances in the child's data across time periods?

4. What are the formal, semantic and syntactic characteristics of modals in caregivers' data across time periods and how are these related to the corresponding characteristics in the child's data across time periods?

5. What factors are at work and how they interact on modal acquisition?

2.7 Summary

Modal verbs are a set of grammatical functors that express a set of related notions such as desire, volition, ability, permission, obligation, and possibility and necessity. Modality in Chinese and English may generally represent the same concept but have variations across the two languages, possibly due to their prominence, information load, etc. There is a rich literature on the acquisition of modality in English, whereas there are only two studies on Chinese modal acquisition. The present study will investigate the early development of formal, semantic and syntactic aspects of Chinese modal verbs in the speech of a single child Q from 1; 4 to 3; 3, and then discuss factors constraining modal acquisition process.

Methodology

The research methods one employs may be a matter of personal preference, but the choice of method is also determined in large part by the questions one seeks answers to, the body of knowledge that already exists on that topic, the domain of inquiry and context, and the methods the questions lend themselves to (Duff 2008). The case study research design is adopted in the present study because the characteristic strengths of case study make this methodology most suitable in studying the early acquisition of Chinese modality. The present chapter is devoted to the presentation of the rationale for conducting a disciplined case-study and the description of my own case-study investigation of the early modal development of one subject from 1; 4 to 3; 3.

3.1 Case-study Methodology

3.1.1 Defining Case Study

Case study has been defined in numerous different ways, most definitions of case study highlight the bounded, singular nature of the case, the importance of context, the availability of multiple sources of information or perspectives on observations, and the in-depth nature of analysis. Creswell (1998) and Merriam (1998), respectively, phrase it somewhat differently:

> A case study is an exploration of a "bounded system" or a case (or multiple cases) over time through detailed, in-depth data

collection involving multiple sources of information rich in context. (Creswell 1998: 61)

The qualitative case study can be defined as an intensive, holistic description and analysis of a single entity, phenomenon, or social unit. Case studies are particularistic, descriptive, and heuristic and rely heavily on inductive reasoning in handling multiple data sources. (Merriam 1998: 16)

The purpose of case study is to understand the complexity and dynamic nature of the particular entity, and to discover systematic connections among experiences, behaviors, and relevant features of the context (Johnson 1992: 84). This emphasis on complexity and of a holistic understanding of the individual's knowledge or performance is foregrounded in recent reviews of the philosophy of science (Larsen- Freeman 1997; van Lier 1997, 2004), which point out that "in complex nonlinear systems, the behavior of the whole emerges out of the interaction of its parts. Studying the parts in isolation one by one will tell us about each part, but not how they interact" (Larsen-Freeman 1997: 157).

3.1.2   Advantages and Disadvantages of Case Study

Case study methodology is often contrasted, negatively, with large-scale experimental methods. The strengths of one approach tend to be the weaknesses of the other. According to Shaughnessy and Zechmeister (1985), the goals, methods, and types of information obtained from the two approaches are simply different.

Case studies have a number of characteristics that make them attractive. First of all, when done well, case studies have a high degree of completeness, depth of analysis, and readability (Nunan 1992). Since case studies concentrate on the behavior of one individual or a small number of individuals, it is possible to conduct a very thorough analysis (a "thick" or "rich" description) of the case and to include triangulated perspectives from other participants or observers.

Besides, case study may provide considerable primary data, which enable readers to get to know the cases well and to consider corroborating cases or counter-examples.

Secondly, the case study method is helpful in generating hypotheses and in suggesting extended research (Gerring 2001). Piaget formulates his theory of human cognitive development while watching his own two children as they passed from childhood to adulthood. Halliday (1973) discoveres that children's early communicative system has six functional categories by studying the language development of his own son from 0; 9 to 2; 6. Tomasello (1992) put forward the famous "verb island hypothesis" through investigating the acquisition process of verbs by his daughter in her second year of life. Case studies may be more useful than cross-sectional studies when a subject is being encountered for the first time or is being considered in a fundamentally new way. The hypotheses or models generated by case studies can be tested later, using the same or other research design, such as a larger cross-sectional design, experimentation, meta-analyses or meta-synthesis, computer modeling, or additional case studies.

Thirdly, longitudinal case study research helps to confirm stages or transformations proposed on the basis of larger (e.g. cross-sectional) studies and provides developmental evidence that can otherwise only be inferred (Duff 2008: 47).

In spite of the benefits of pioneering, in-depth case study research described above, several features often considered weaknesses or limitations should be noted. The first and most pronounced of these disadvantages is related to generalizability. This limitation of case study reflects a historic rift in the philosophy of science. In one camp are the proponents of quantitative research, who seek to make broad generalizations from which to formulate general laws or principles; in the other are the proponents of qualitative research, whose focus may be the individual—that which is unique, rather than that which is common (Shaughnessy & Zechmeister 1985). However, some qualitative researchers consider that theory in case studies can help in generalizing the results to other cases. A term that is commonly substituted for generalizability in the qualitative literature is transferability—of hypotheses, principles, or findings (Lincoln & Guba 1985). Transferability assigns the responsibility of determining whether there is a congruence, fit, or connection between one study context and their own context to readers, but it does not have the original researchers make that assumption for them.

Another criticism sometimes leveled against the case study method is that it lacks objectivity: researchers might have preconceived notions or biases when undertaking research or that they might identify too closely with their case participants and lose all perspective (Duff 2008: 55). The claim of subjectivity is true to some extent, but could also be leveled against much research of all types. In fact, all research involves personal judgment in making research decisions, framing studies based on earlier research, and drawing interpretations and conclusions, although some research may have more procedures in place to establish reliability. Many interpretive qualitative researchers question whether researchers can be truly objective in the human and social sciences (Yin 2003; Miles & Huberman 1994: 262). They suggest that it is invaluable to be candid and reflective about one's own subjectivities, biases (ideologies), and engagement with research participants and with the research itself. Furthermore, it would allay concerns about unprincipled subjectivity if researchers could provid sufficient details about decision making, coding or analysis, chains of reasoning, and data sampling.

In addition, since case studies include considerable details and contextualization about the person, site, or event featured, it is very difficult to protect the identity of the participants, even when pseudonyms are used (Duff 2008: 59).

3.1.3   Justification for the Application of Case Study Method

The strengths of case study render it a suitable means to the exploration of Chinese modality acquisition process.

The case study approach is suitable for studying very complex, context-bounded, and highly dynamic processes (Halliday 1975; Rist 1977; Shallice 1979; Stake 1978, 1981; Dromi 1987; Tomasello 1992, etc.). Dromi (1987: 64) notes that two characteristics of early speech make case-study methodology the suitable choice for a research paradigm in this realm: (a) during the early periods of production the linguistic knowledge of the child changes quickly and constantly (e.g. Braunwald 1978; Nelson & Lucariello 1985); and (b) early verbal productions are strongly dependent on their linguistic and non-linguistic contexts (e.g. Bates 1976; Clark 1982; Peters 1983).

Peters (1983: 87) and Clark (1982) state that experimental conditions contain tasks which are too simplified and too isolated from the regular experiences of toddlers, and therefore they are too constraining for very young children. Young children tend to show high levels of stress during testing and sometimes manifest low performance because they are restricted by the questions and the instructions. Besides, since a child's early expressions are very telegraphic, a close familiarity with the subject and his or her non-linguistic experiences is a necessary condition for correct interpretation (Rodgon 1976; Braunwald & Brislin 1979).

Literature on the acquisition of Chinese modality is scarce, and little is known about the trajectory of the acquisition process. Systematic and in-depth case study would be more helpful than cross-sectional studies in discovering the acquisition path.

3.2   The Subject and Settings

The subject of this investigation is my daughter Q —a first born and only child. Q was born and brought up in Guangzhou City while all of her caretakers, parents and grandparents, are from Henan province. Her caretakers spoke Henan dialect among themselves and spoke Mandarin to Q. The phonology of Henan dialect is different from Mandarin while the grammar systems of the two are almost the same. Q could understand the Henan dialect when her caretakers are talking in that dialect but she has rarely learned how to speak it, probably because all her caretakers interact with her only in Mandarin. Q's father was a PhD candidate in linguistics when this investigation started.

Q was 1; 4.11 at the beginning of data collection. On the last day of recording, Q was 3; 3.17. The natural speech data were collected when Q was playing in the course of spontaneous interactions with her caretakers or her playmates. I stayed with Q for at least 4 hours a day when she was awake and I was the major observer-recorder of the data, while her father recorded the data sporadically. Most of the data were collected at home, which is an apartment located on the campus of Guangdong University of Foreign Studies. Some of the data were recorded on the campus while we were out for a walk, or during shopping or social activities with our friends. The following sections describe the specific procedures employed in collecting the data.

3.3   Data-collection Procedures

A case-study investigation of early speech must be distinct from a mere collection of anecdotes about specific speech events (Dromi 1987: 64). When a child is observed selectively and/or randomly, transient and short-lived phenomena can be noted and mistakenly interpreted as representative of a typical and regularly occurring linguistic behavior. In a selective method of data collection, the examples noted may be irregular or limited only to those which best accord with the researcher's hypothesis. Therefore, the researcher undertaking a case-study must commit himself to an ongoing and intensive data-collection process.

The inclusion of various means for collecting the information is also recommended in order to establish a broad-spectrum record. Using multiple sources of data allows researchers to "corroborate and augment evidence from other sources" (Yin 2003: 87). The current study involves data from the handwritten diary, transcripts of audio-and video-recordings.

3.3.1   The Handwritten Diary

Diary studies have provided ground-breaking work for our understanding of children's language acquisition. Among the earliest studies of child language acquisition, Stern and Stern (1928/1975, cited in Müller 1998) use diaries to document young German-speaking children's early productions. More recently, on the basis of a diary of his daughter's earliest verb uses, Tomasello (1992) argue that children's early linguistic knowledge may be constructed around verb island before children learn to generalize schemas across several verbs. Diary studies can document with extensive details the earliest signs of language comprehension and production in children. The parent-researcher sees a much wider range of real-life situations than is possible for researchers who make weekly visits. The spontaneous data produced by the child outside of recording sessions can be captured, partially if not exhaustively (Braunwald & Brislin 1979; Mervis, Mervis, Johnson et al. 1992). Besides, even in the age of video and computer technologies, diary studies have an important role to play since having a relatively complete record for a single child's language allows us to ask important questions that periodic records from a larger population simply do not permit (Mervis, Mervis, Johnson, et al. 1992). However, the problems with diary studies are that researchers might be able to write down only partial and inaccurate information due to the fast progress of interaction and that handwritten notes cannot be verified by other researchers. These shortcomings have been addressed in more recent years by complementing handwritten notes with audio- and/or video-recordings (Lieven, Behrens, Spears, et al. 2003).

The diary record of Q's linguistic development constitutes the main source of data in the present investigation. I kept a diary in the house and carried with me a note pad when we left the house. Any notes taken away from the house were transferred to the main diary in the evening of the day they were recorded. The diary includes extensive information about Q's linguistic behavior throughout a total period of almost 24 months. During this period, most of Q's utterances of modality were noted down, accompanied by detailed and systematic descriptions of linguistic and non-linguistic contexts in which they were produced.

3.3.2 The Audio-recordings

In order to obtain supplementary sources of evidence, Q's interaction with her caretakers and playmates were audio-recorded for about twice every week. The recorded sessions ranged in length from 10 to 60 minutes, with an average length of about 30 minutes. There are a total of 293 files and about 850 minutes audio-recordings. These data were collected in order to compensate for the drawbacks of the procedures that are typical for the recording of selective examples by pre-planned criteria. The recordings provide a rich source of data on the characteristics of the mother's linguistic input to the child and the patterns of interaction between the mother and the child.

The audio-recorded sessions took place either at home or on the campus. The recording equipment used was recording pen (Samsung YV-120), which I placed on a table near Q when we were at home or I carried it in my hand when we were out.

3.3.3 The Video-recordings

Video-recordings were planned as an additional source of data that would document not only the audible components of situations but also their visual aspects so that non-linguistic contexts of the interactions could be better captured. Q's interaction with her caretakers and playmates were video-recorded for about once every two weeks, and the length of the video-recording sessions range in length from about 10 minutes to 60 minutes, with the average length of about 30 minutes. There is a total of 258 files and about 3200 minutes video-recordings. The video-recorded sessions took place in our home or on the campus. The equipment used was Digital Camera Recorder (Sony DCR-SR60E).

3.4 Data Transcription and Analysis

Due to lack of time and labor, only part of audio- and video-recordings were transcribed. About 60-minute recordings (mainly video recordings) in each month were first transcribed by about 30 juniors in Guangdong University of Foreign Studies majoring in linguistics, and then checked by me. Exhaustive transcripts were made and stored in the CHAT Transcription Format (Codes for the Human Analysis of Transcripts) (MacWhinney 2009), which is the standard transcription system for the CHILDES (Child Language Data Exchange System) Project. The child's and other participants' utterances in the present study were transcribed with information about situations, contexts, and gestures. File names followed the format of D (A, V) year; month, day, with D, A, V standing for diary data, audio recordings and video recordings respectively, and year;

month; day standing for the exact age of the child. For example, file name D 1; 8.24 shows the transcription is from the diary data when the child was 1 year 8 months and 24 days old, and similarly, V 1; 5.15 shows the transcription is from the video recording when the child was 1 year 5 months and 15 days old. Unless stated, all the data investigated in the present study are from recordings, while diary data, which were detailed record of modal utterances by the child on daily bases, were only used as backup for more detailed information. For the ease of analyzing, the whole corpus of audio and video recordings was divided into eight 2-month periods corresponding to the child's age as is shown in Table 3-1.

Table 3-1　Time periods of audio and video recordings

Time period	Age
Period 1	1; 4 to 1; 6
Period 2	1; 7 to 1; 9
Period 3	1; 10 to 2; 0
Period 4	2; 1 to 2; 3
Period 5	2; 4 to 2; 6
Period 6	2; 7 to 2; 9
Period 7	2; 10 to 3; 0
Period 8	3; 1 to 3; 3

In China, most mothers would go back to work after their babies get 6 months old, therefore maternal or paternal grandparents would move in with the family to take care of babies until they are old enough for kindergarten or even primary school. As a result, the linguistic input from both the parents and the grandparents need to be studied to investigate the influence input might have on the language acquision process of the child. The subject of the present study, Qianqian, was taken care of by her parents, her maternal grandparents and paternal grandparents in turn. The input data would thus include all the modal utterances by the six caregivers. Utterances that include the target modal verbs were selected automatically with the KWAL (keyword and line) program in CLAN, which is the analyzing tool of CHAT format files. For the present study, spontaneous uses of modal utterances were examined. Imitations were excluded from the study. Utterances in which the child immediately repeated the exact modal utterances produced by the adult were considered imitations[1]. The modal utterances by the child Qian Qian and all her caregivers in the data (diary data, audio and video recordings) were coded in the following three ways (due to lack of labor, codings were made by myself, and when ambiguities arise I consulted with another PhD student specializing in modal acquisition until complete agreement was reached):

(a) *Basic functional coding*

It indicated modals' domain and function, which was determined on the basis of its meaning and linguistic and situational context. All modals were classified as dynamic modals (intention, desire, ability), deontic modals (obligation, permission, prohibition, necessity) or epistemic modals (possibility, necessity). Take the functional coding of modal 要 *yào* 'want/must' and 能 *néng* 'can' for example:

(1) (The child walks toward the little pidgeon) D 2; 5.25

    *CHI: 我　　要　　抱　　　小鸽子。

        Wǒ　*yào*　*bào*　　*xiǎogēzi.*

        I　　want　hug　　little pidgeon

        'I want to hug little pidgeon.'

---

1 Modal utterances by the child like 想 *xiǎng* '(I) want to (ride a horse)' as an anwer to daddy's question 想不想骑马呀 *xiǎng bù xiǎng qí mǎ ya* 'do you want to ride a horse or not' are not considered as imitations, because Chinese adults produce lots of interrogatives in the form of [Mod +不 *bú* 'not' + Mod] construction (想不想 *xiǎng bù xiǎng* 'desire not desire', 会不会 *huì bú huì* 'can not can', 要不要 *yào bú yào* 'want not want', 敢不敢 *gǎn bù gǎn* 'dare not dare', 用不用 *yòng bú yòng* 'need not need', 愿不愿意 *yuàn bú yuànyì* 'willing not willing', 能不能 *néng bù néng* 'can not can', 可不可以 *kě bù kěyǐ* 'may not may', 该不该 *gāi bù gāi* 'should not should' and 喜不喜欢 *xǐ bù xǐhuān* 'like not like'), and it is very natural for the child to answer these questions with bare positive or negative modal forms (想/不想 *xiǎng/bù xiǎng* 'desire/not desire', 会/不会 *huì/bú huì* 'can/can not'. 要/不要 *yào/ bú yào* 'want/not want', 敢/不敢 *gǎn/bù gǎn* 'dare/not dare', 用/不用 *yòng/bú yòng* 'need/not need', 愿意/不愿意 *yuànyì/bú yuànyì* 'willing/not willing', 能/不能 *néng/bù néng* 'can/can not', 可以/不可以 *kěyǐ/bù kěyǐ* 'may/may not', 该/不该 *gāi/bù gāi* 'should/not should', 喜欢/不喜欢 *xǐhuān/bù xǐhuān* 'like/not like').

(2) (The child reaches a box on the book shelf) D 2; 5.30

*CHI: 我　　能　　够着　　了。

Wǒ　　néng　gòuzháo　le.

I　　can　　reach　　PHA

'I can reach (the box) now. '

(3) (Mommy is walking with high-heel shoes) D 2; 7.18

*CHI: 妈妈　　　要　　　小心。

Māma　　　yào　　xiǎoxīn.

mommy　　must　　careful

'Mommy must be careful.'

(4) (Grandpa is walking toward the child) D 2; 1.11

*CHI: 爷爷　　不　　能　　进　　屋。

Yéye　　bù　　néng　jìn　　wū.

grandpa　not　can　enter　room

'Grandpa, do not enter the room.'

(5) (Wind blows through the leaves) D 2; 3.30

*CHI: 要　　下雨　　了。

Yào　　xiàyǔ　le.

must　　rain　　PHA

'It's going to rain.'

(6) (The child is watching catoon with mommy) D 2; 9.10

*CHI: 老妖婆　　光　　把　　　　　　你　　吃掉。

Lǎoyāopó　guāng　bǎ　　　　　nǐ　　chīdiào.

evil spirit　will　Executive Marker　you　　eat

'The evil spirit will eat you.'

*MOT: 老妖婆　　在　哪儿?

Lǎoyāopó　zài　nǎ'er?

evil spirit　is　where

'Where is the evil spirit?'

*CHI: 电视　　　里。
　　　Diànshì　　*lǐ.*
　　　TV　　　　in
　　　'In the TV.'

*MOT: 那　　她　　怎么　　能　　把　　　　　　　　　我
　　　Nà　　*tā*　　*zěnme*　*néng*　*bǎ*　　　　　　　*wǒ*
　　　then　she　how　　can　Executive Marker　me
　　　吃掉　　　呢?
　　　chīdiào　*ne?*
　　　eat　　　P
　　　'Then how can she eat me?'.

The 要 *yào* 'want' in (1) and the 能 *néng* 'can' in (2) are coded as dynamic modals, since 要 *yào* 'want' expresses the child's strong desire to hold the little pigeon and the 能 *néng* 'can' expresses the child's ability to reach the box. The 要 *yào* 'must' in example (3) and the 能 *néng* 'can' in (4) are coded as deontic modals, since 要 *yào* 'must' expresses mommy's obligation to be careful and 能 *néng* 'can' expresses the child's prohibition on grandpa's actions. The 要 *yào* 'want' in (5) and the 能 *néng* 'can' in (6) are coded as epistemic modals, since the 要 *yào* 'want' expresses the child's prediction about the weather and the 能 *néng* 'can' expresses the possibility of certain occurrence.

(b) *Coding of referents for modal subjects*

Modals were coded as to whether the subject of the modal pertained to the self, to another person, or to neither. It should be noted that 我们 *wǒmen* 'we' was coded as referring to the self. 他/她 *tā* 'he/she' and 弟弟/妹妹 *dìdi/mèimei* 'younger brother/younger sister' referring to dolls were coded as referring to another person since the child treated dolls like they are human beings when playing house with them as in (7). Neither generally captured uses that pertained to the physical world as in (5), and uses that pertained to animals as in (8).

(7) (The child is playing house with a little doll) V 2; 4.12

*CHI: 她　　想　　　尿。

Tā　　xiǎng　　niào.

she　　want　　pee

'She wants to pee.'

%act: 把小娃娃抱到厕所 (take the little doll to the toilet)

(8) (Mommy prohibits the child from touching the fish's mouth)
D 2; 4.01

*CHI: 鱼　　会　　咬　　手。

Yú　　huì　　yǎo　　shǒu.

fish　　may　　bit　　hand

'The fish may bite (my) hand.'

(c) *Coding of sentence types*

Utterances containing modals were coded as affirmatives, negatives and questions.

If a modal could not be interpreted clearly enough to permit classification of all three dimensions (even after referring back to the entire transcript if necessary), it was coded as uninterpretable. For example:

(9) (The child is chatting with mommy) D 2; 4.01

*CHI: 龙眼　　是　山魈　　　摘　　的　　吗?

Lóngyǎn　　shì　shānxiào　　zhāi　　de　　ma?

longan　　is　　mandrill　　pick　　P　　P?

'Are longans picked by the mandrills?'

*MOT: 香蕉　　是 大象　　摘 的, 龙眼　是　小 猴子 摘的。

Xiāngjiāo shì dàxiàng zhāi de, lóngyǎn shì xiǎo hóuzi zhāi de.

banana is elephant pick P longan is little monkey pick P

'Bananas are picked by the elephants, and longans are picked by the little monkeys.'

> *CHI: 大象　　会　#　摘　#　香蕉　　给　我　吃。
> *Dàxiàng huì zhāi xiāngjiāo gěi wǒ chī.*
> elephant can pick banana give me eat
> 'The elephants can pick bananas for me.'

The 会 *huì* 'can' in 大象会摘香蕉给我吃 *dàxiàng huì zhāi xiāngjiāo gěi wǒ chī* 'The elephants can pick bananas for me' can be classified as a dynamic modal expressing certain ability possessed by the elephants or as an epistemic modal expressing possible actions performed by the elephants. Since both interpretations are possible in the above conversation, the 会 *huì* 'can' is coded as uninterpretable.

Chapter 4

Features of Modals in the Child's Data and in the Caregivers' Data

This chapter presents the results with respect to each of the research questions. The formal, semantic and syntactic features of modals in the child's data and in the caregivers' data are investigated respectively and then compared.

4.1 The Acquisition of Modal Forms in the Child's Data

Research question 1 is answered by tracing the emergence as well as developmental patterns of Chinese modal forms in the child's data across time periods.

4.1.1 The Emergence of Chinese Modal Forms in the Child's Data

This section aims to examine the age of emergence of modal verbs in the child's data. The following table shows the child's age at the first appearance[1] of modal verbs. The data are from the diary data, audio and video transcriptions.

As is shown in Table 4-1, modal verbs emerged gradually from

1　Some studies on modal acquisition regard the ages of the first occurrence of modals as the starting point of acquisition, while others regard the ages of the third occurrence of modals as the starting point of acquisition. The present study regards the ages of the first occurrence of modals as the starting point of acquisition, and the ages of the third occurrence of modals are provided in appendix 1, which might be useful for researchers to make comparisons with their studies.

the end of 1; 8 to 2; 4, and modal utterances developed from answers to caregivers' questions in bare modal forms to spontaneous utterances in complete sentences. The first modal form emerged was 想 *xiǎng* at the end of 1; 8, in isolated use as an answer to daddy's question 你想不想骑马 *nǐ xiǎng bù xiǎng qímǎ* 'do you want to ride a horse'. The second modal emerged was 会 *huì* in isolated use as an answer to grandpa's question 你会不会 (开 DVD) *nǐ huì bú huì (kāi DVD)* 'can you (turn on the DVD)'. The following modals mainly (six in eleven occurrences) occurred in the child's spontaneous speech, as in 妈妈不要写 *māma bú yào xiě* 'don't write, mommy' when the child wanted mommy to stop writing. Most modals first appeared in their positive forms, whereas 要 *yào* and 敢 *gǎn* first appeared in their negative forms. More information on the first occurrence of modals is provided in Appendix 1.

Erbaugh (1982) notes that 会 *huì* 'know how to' was the first modal that emerged in children's speech, which appeared during 1; 10 to 2; 4. For one child Pang, 会 *huì* 'know how to' first appeared in isolation as an answer to an adult question, followed by the bare negative form 不会 *bú huì* 'not know how to' as an answer to the adult question, and then 会 *huì* 'know how to' and 不会 *bú huì* 'not know how to' were used with complements in spontaneous utterances. During 2; 6 to 3; 2, modals 能 *néng* 'can', 可以 *kěyǐ* 'able to, may', 敢 *gǎn* 'dare' and 应该 *yīng gāi* 'should' appeared in spontaneous declarative speech. Where they were used, the appropriate modal was generally selected. The first modal emerged in Q's data was 想 *xiǎng* 'desire', followed by 会 *huì* 'know how to'. Similar to Erbaugh's observations, these two modals also first appeared in isolation in answer to adults' questions and then in spontaneous speech. The age of first emergence of modals recorded by the present study, however, is about one month earlier than that recorded by Erbaugh's investigation. Different subjects as well as different sampling methods between the two studies might have resulted in the age gap of modal acquisition. Pang is taciturn, while Q is talkative. Erbaugh audiotaped hour-long visits with Pang since she was 1; 10 every two weeks, whereas the present study traced the ontogenesis of modals in Q's speech since she was 1; 4 on daily basis.

Table 4-1   The first occurrence of Chinese modal forms in the child's data

Modal forms	First utterance	Age
想 *xiǎng*	想 *xiǎng* '(I) want to (ride a horse).'	1; 8.27
会 *huì*	会 *huì* '(I) can (turn on the DVD).'	1; 8.29
要 *yào*	妈妈不要写 *māma bú yào xiě* 'mommy, do not write.'	1; 9.13
敢 *gǎn*	不敢尝 *bù gǎn cháng* '(I) dare not taste it.'	1; 9.25
用 *yòng*	用吧 *yòng ba* '(I) need (hold your hand)!'	1; 9.28
愿意 *yuànyì*	愿意 *yuànyì* '(I'm) willing to.'	1; 10.04
能 *néng*	妈妈能扶 *māma néng fú* 'mommy can hold it.'	1; 10.22
可以 *kěyǐ*	可以 *kěyǐ* 'you may (take the doll away).'	1; 11.22
该 *gāi*	该吃饭了 *gāi chī fàn le* 'It's time to eat.'	1; 11.29
得 *děi*	得小心点 *děi xiǎoxīn diǎn* 'I have to be careful.'	2; 2.03
喜欢 *xǐhuan*	我喜欢摸摸它 *wǒ xǐ·huān mōmo tā* 'I like petting it.'	2; 4.12

Studies on the acquisition of English modals converge on the finding that modal forms *can't/can* are the first modals that emerged, followed by *won't/will*. Wells' (1979) study with 60 children shows that the first modal form acquired by children were *can/can't* at 2; 3 (at least 50% of the children in the sample), followed by *will* at 2; 6. Stephany (1986) observes that the first modal form emerged in eight English-speaking children's data was *can't*, and only when *can* was separated from its negative element do *will*, *won't*, and *should* appear. Contrary to Stephany's findings, Shatz, Billman, and Yaniv's (1986) examination of more than 3,500 utterances produced by 30 children reveals *can* and *will* were the first modals most frequently appearing in children's speech. They note negative modal constructions, although common, are not necessarily the first forms children use. Studies on modal acquisition both in Chinese and in English seem to show that modal forms expressing ability and intention are acquired first. In the case of Chinese modal acquisition, 会 *huì* 'know how to' and 想 *xiǎng* 'desire' are acquired first which express ability and intention respectively. In the case of English modal acquisition, *can't/can* and *won't/will* are acquired first which express ability and intention respectively.

In comparison with the age of emergence of other word categories, such as nouns and verbs, modals emerge late in children's speech. Modal utterances usually emerge in children's spontaneous speech from 2; 0 to 2; 6, which is about 1 year later than the utterance of the first word. Why do modals emerge late and develop gradually? Factors contributing to the late emergence and gradual acquisition of modals are discussed as follows.

Modals are a complex system, which put higher demands on children's cognitive ability. First of all, modals are semantically abstract, which makes it difficult for children to acquire. Words referring to concrete objects or actions, such as concrete nouns and verbs, always emerge early. Modals, in contrast, emerge late because they do not have concrete referents and therefore present greater challenge for children to acquire. Presumably, it would be easier to acquire the word 水 *shuǐ* 'water' than the word 会 *huì* 'know how to, may' since the latter is semantically vague and abstract. Similarly, it would be easier to acquire the word *sheep* than the word *would*.

Secondly, the modal system is semantically complex, which may have resulted in their late emergence and gradual acquisition. The modal system is a very complex system, and there exist minute differences among modal forms. For instance, dynamic modals 想 *xiǎng* 'desire' and 要 *yào* 'want' both express the notion of desire. 想 *xiǎng* 'desire' denotes weak desire, whereas 要 *yào* 'want' denotes strong desire. Deontic modals 要 *yào* 'must', 该 *gāi* 'should' and 得 *děi* 'have to' all express the notion of obligation. 要 *yào* 'must' often occurs in its negative form 不要 *bú yào* 'not must' denoting prohibition on others' action, 该 *gāi* 'should' denoting obligation based on routine, whereas 得 *děi* 'have to' denoting obligation of neutral or negative attitude in speech. Epistemic modals 会 *huì* 'may' and 要 *yào* 'must' both express the speaker's estimation on possible/probable occurrences. 会 *huì* 'may' denotes epistemic possibility, whereas 要 *yào* 'must' denots epistemic necessity.

Thirdly, modals are usually placed after subjects and before main verbs, which means that only when subject-verb-object constructions have been acquired will modals emerge. Q started to produce complete sentences when she entered 1; 8. For example, Q uttered 爸爸坐坐 *bàba zuòzuo* 'daddy sit' while patting on the stair where she was sitting on, asking daddy to sit besides her (D 1; 8.09). For another example, Q said 爸爸开门 *bàba kāi mén* 'Daddy opens the door' while holding daddy's hand and walking towards the closed door to let daddy help her open the door (V 1; 8.13). At the end of 1; 8, about 20 days later than the emergence of subject-verb-object constructions, Q started to produce modal utterances containing 想 *xiǎng* 'desire' and 会 *huì* 'know how to'.

The above discussion shows that modals are a very complex system semantically and syntactically. The linguistic complexities of modals put higher demands on children's cognitive abilities, which might have led to their later acquisition. To what extent is caregiver input related to late modal acquisition will be discussed in detail in 4.5.

Studies on the acquisition of English modals show that English modals emerge around 2; 0. The present study and Erbaugh's study, however, suggest that Chinese modals emerge earlier than that of English modals. What factors might have led to the earlier emergence of Chinese modals?

The fact that some Chinese modals can also be used as main verbs might have prompted the earlier emergence of their modal uses. Modals 想 *xiǎng* 'desire', 会 *huì* 'know how to, may', 要 *yào* 'want, must', 用 *yòng* 'need to', 愿意 *yuànyì* 'willing', 该 *gāi* 'should', 得 *děi* 'have to, must' and 喜欢 *xǐhuān* 'like' can be used as main verbs. 想 *xiǎng* refers to 'the action of thinking' or 'miss' with nominal or clausal complement, e.g., 想办法 *xiǎng bàn fǎ* 'thinking about the solution', 想家 *xiǎng jiā* 'miss hometown' (Modern Chinese Dictionary: 1376). 会 *huì* means 'know' or 'meet' with nominal complement, e.g., 会英文 *huì yīngwén* 'know English', 会友 *huì yǒu* 'meet a friend' (ibid: 565-566). 要 *yào* means 'to desire to have the possession of' with nominal complement, e.g., 他要一个口琴 *tā yào yī gè kǒuqín* 'He asks for a harmonia' (ibid: 1456). 用 *yòng* means 'to use' with nominal complement, e.g., 用力 *yòng lì* 'use energy', 用心 *yòng xīn* 'at pains' (ibid: 1518). 愿意 *yuànyì* means 'wish, expect' with a clausal complemtent[1], e.g., 他们愿意你留在这里 *tāmen yuànyì nǐ liú zài zhèlǐ* 'They wish that you could stay here' (ibid: 1554). 该 *gāi* means 'should' or 'owe' with nominal compliment, e.g., 这一回该我了吧 *zhè yī huí gāi wǒ le bā* 'It should be my turn this time', 该帐 *gāi zhàng* 'owe money' (ibid: 401). According to Lü (1980) the main verb use of 得 *děi* is 'a quantity-word taking verb', which takes a number referring to the quantity of the things required as its complement, e.g., 这个工程得三个月才能完 *zhège gōngchéng děi sān ge yuè cái néng wán* 'It takes three months to complete this project'(ibid: 263). 喜欢 *xǐhuān* means 'like' with nominal complement, e.g., 我喜欢数学 *wǒ xǐhuan shùxué* 'I like mathematics' (ibid: 1350).

From Table 4-2, we can see that 想 *xiǎng* 'the action of thinking, miss', 要 *yào* 'to desire to have the possession of', 用 *yòng* 'to use' and 喜欢 *xǐ huān* 'like' were used as main verbs in the child's data. 要 *yào* 'to desire to have the possession of' was first used as a main verb at 1; 5.15 in a single declarative when the child reached out her hand for a balloon in mommy's hand, which was about 4 months earlier than its first modal use. Similar to 要 yào 'to desire to have the possession of',

---

1 Both Lü (1980) and Chao (1968) point out this main verb use of 愿意 *yuànyì*, which is a marginal use of this word.

the main verb use of 喜欢 *xǐhuān* 'like' appeared 3 months earlier than its modal use. The main verb uses, however, did not always precede the modal uses. For example, the main verb uses of 想 *xiǎng* 'the action of thinking, miss' and 用 *yòng* 'to use' appeared later than their modal uses. Therefore, not all the main verb uses have prompted their modal uses.

Table 4-2 The first occurrence of main verb uses of target forms in the child's data

Forms	First utternaces	Age
想 *xiǎng*	妈妈想芊芊 *māma xiǎng qiānqian* 'mommy miss Qian Qian'	D 1; 9.10
会 *huì*	✕	✕
要 *yào*	要（气球）*yào qìqíu* '(I) want to have (the balloon)'	V 1; 5.15
用 *yòng*	我用一下（盒子）*wǒ yòng yī xià (hézi)* 'I use (the box) once '	D 2; 0.21
愿意 *yuàn yì*	✕	✕
该 *gāi*	✕	✕
得 *děi*	✕	✕
喜欢 *xǐhuān*	芊芊喜欢大灰狼 *Qiān Qiān xǐhuān dàhuīláng* 'Qian Qian likes the big wolf'	D 2; 1.22

The second factor that may have prompted the earlier emergence of Chinese modals could be related to the [Modal+不 *bù* 'not' +Modal] question construction often observed in Chinese caregivers' speech and the quiz style of conversation for Chinese. Since children tend to pay attention to the end of sentences, the [Modal+不 *bù* 'not' +Modal] question construction might have contributed partly to the earlier emergence of Chinese modal forms. It was noticed that the first two modals emerged in the child's data 想 *xiǎng* 'desire' and 会 *huì* 'know how to' were first isolated uses in answers to adult questions 你想不想骑马 *nǐ xiǎng bù xiǎng qímǎ* 'Do you want to ride a horse' and 你会不会 *nǐ huì bú huì* 'Can you do it' before spontaneous uses. Erbaugh (1982) also observes that children started to use modal auxiliaries 会 *huì* 'know how to' and 要 *yào* 'want' between 1; 10 to 2; 4, and the two modals remained rare except in answer to adult questions. Erbaugh notes that the quiz style of conversation for Chinese facilitates Chinese modal acquisition. Studies on epistemic modal acquisition of other languages also show that linguistic salience may favour the early acquisition of epistemic divices.

A third factor contributing to the earlier emergence of Chinese modals in comparision with that of English modals might be that verbs are priviledged in Chinese while nouns are priviledged in English. Over the past decades, several studies of Mandarin- and Cantonese-speaking children's early vocabulary development have provided converging evidence for the fact that Chinese-speaking children's vocabularies contain a much higher proportion of verbs and English-speaking children's vocabularies contain a much higher proportion of nouns (Tardif 1996; Tardif, Gelman & Xu 1999; Tardif et al. 2002).

Tardif (1996) examined the productive vocabularies of ten 22-month- old toddlers who were recorded for one hour each in naturalistic contexts together with their caregivers in their own homes, and results show that nine of these ten children who were able to produce any nouns or verbs produced more verbs than nouns. Tardif, Gelman & Xu (1999) conducted another laboratory study which controlled activity contexts and matched English- and Mandarin-speaking samples, which reveals that English-speaking children produced higher proportions of nouns and lower proportions of verbs than the Mandarin-speaking children. Tardif et al. (2002) conducted a large-scale standardization study of the MacArthur Communicative Development Inverntory (CDI)[1] (Fenson et al. 1993) in both Mandarin

---

1 The MacArthur Communicative Development Inventory (CDI) is a standardised parent reporting system used to assess monolingual children's lexical growth. The CDI comes in two scales: the infant scale (covering the period from 8 to 16 months) and the toddler scale (from 16 to 30 months). The infant scale looks at comprehension, word production and aspects of symbolic and communicative gesture. The toddler scale examines word production and the early phases of grammar. The CDI requires parents or caretakers to report on their children's progress by observing them for periods lasting between 15 and 45 minutes. For the infant scale, during these observation sessions the parents/caretakers match words comprehended and spontaneously produced by the children in separate columns. For the toddler scale, the parents/caretakers match the number of words repeatedly produced by the children with those on the CDI scale.

and Cantonese, for which they interviewed over 1, 600 mothers and other primary caregivers of 8- to 30-month-old infants and toddlers in Beijing and Hong Kong respectively. As with the naturalistic data, the large sample CDI results show clear noun-verb differences between children who were learning English versus those learning Mandarin or Cantonese. From the studies conducted above, one is left with the conclusion that under any given context or measurement method, Chinese-speaking children produce and have access to a much higher proportion of verbs than English-speaking children.

As with children's data, Mandarin-speaking adults produced a much higher proportion of verbs in their speech than their English-speaking counterparts (Tardif 1997; Tardif, Gelman & Xu 1999; Tardif & Fu in preparation). Tardif, Shatz & Naigles (1997) investigated the adult-to-child speech of English-, Italian-, and Mandarin-speaking caregivers. They discover that Mandarin speakers used relatively more verb tokens and verb types. In contrast, the English- and Italian- speakers used roughly equal numbers of noun and verb types, and both groups used more verb tokens than noun tokens, but not as many as the Mandarin speakers. In the second study (Tardif, Gelman & Xu 1999), both the children's and the caregivers' speech was limited by the toys and activity contexts that they were asked to participate in. Again, Mandarin-speaking caregivers, like their children, produced relatively fewer nouns and more verbs than the English- speaking caregivers, regardless of which context was measured. In a third study (Tardif & Fu, in preparation), adult-to-adult speech was measured in a time-limited picture description task. As with the studies on child language and adult-to-child language, nouns were more prevalent for the English-speakers and verbs were more prevalent for the Mandarin speakers. Thus, Mandarin-speaking adults not only used verbs more frequently than English speakers in their everyday speech, but they also used a greater variety of verbs than English speakers. Since modal auxiliaries have to be attached to main verbs, the prevalence of verbs in Chinese might favor the earlier acquisition of Chinese modal auxiliaries.

To sum up, Chinese modal forms emerged gradually in the child's speech between 1; 8 and 2; 4. Similar to the findings on the acquisition of English modals, the first Chinese modal forms that emerged expressed the modal notions of ability or intention. The later emergence of modals, as compared with that of nouns or verbs, might have to do with the semantic as well as syntactic complexities of Chinese modal system. The earlier emergence of Chinese modal forms, as compared with that of English modals, might have to do with the facts that some modal forms in Chinese are used as main verbs, the [Modal+不 bù 'not' +Modal] question construction is often observed in caregivers' data, and the prevalence of verbs in Chinese.

4.1.2   Distribution of Modal Forms in the Child's Data Across Time Periods

This section aims to examine the developmental pattern of modal forms in the child's data. Distribution and developmental pattern of modal utterances as well as modal forms will be investigated.

1. Distribution of Modal Utterances in the Child's Data Across Time Periods

In all 432 modal utterances were collected, which represented over 4% of the total sampled utterances. As can be seen from Table 4-3, the percentages of modal utterances in the total utterances across time periods showed a general trend of increase. Modal utterances were non-existent during period 1, and emerged during period 2, which occupied 1% of the total utterances of that period. The percentage remained 1% during period 3 and increased to over 4% during period 4 and 5. The percentage rose to over 7% during period 6, and showed a trend of fluctuations around 7% since then.

Table 4-3   The child's production of utterances and modal utterances
between 1; 4 and 3; 3

	Age	Total no. utterances	Modal utterances	
			No.	% of total
P 1	1; 4 to 1; 6	865	0	0
P 2	1; 7 to 1; 9	925	10	1%
P 3	1; 10 to 2; 0	1 637	17	1%
P 4	2; 1 to 2; 3	867	36	4.1%
P 5	2; 4 to 2; 6	2 331	106	4.5%
P 6	2; 7 to 2; 9	1 412	107	7.5%
P 7	2; 10 to 3; 0	1 124	90	8%
P 8	3; 1 to 3; 3	926	66	7.1%
Total	1; 4 to 3; 3	10 087	432	4.2%

Note: P represents period.

Studies on the acquisition of English modals show that once modals have emerged they are used frequently. The frequency data presented by Wells (1979) indicate that about 9.4% of the utterances of 60 children from 2; 3 to 3; 6 contained auxiliary verbs. Pea and Mawby (1984) find that about 10% of the total utterances by their six subjects, who ranged in age from 2; 4 to 2; 10 and 2; 11 to 3; 5 at the beginning and the end of the observation, contained modals or quasi-modals. Bassano (1996) observes that modal utterances accounted for about 20% of all the utterances by a French-speaking child from 1; 9 to 4; 0. The present study shows that the percentage of modal utterances only accounted for over 4% of the total utterances by the child from 1; 4 to 3; 3, which is much lower than the percentages reported by other researchers. Different scopes of investigation might have in part led to different percentages of modal utterances in the above studies. Wells investigates the acquisition of all auxiliary verbs, including primary auxiliaries, modal auxiliaries as well as quasi-auxiliaries. Primary auxiliaries *be, have* and *do* were the most frequently occurring forms in children's speech in Wells' research, which no doubt increased the percentage of utterances containing auxiliary verbs a lot. Pea and Mawby's study focuses on modals as well as quasi-modals *going to/gonna, got to/gotta, had better, have to, ought to* and *supposed to*, which might also have contributed to the high percentage in their study. Modal utterances in Bassano's study includes all the utterances with the following modal devices in French: modal verbal inflections, modal verbs, main verbs, modal constructions and syntactic particles with modal value. The inclusion of such a wide range of modal devices might have resulted in the high percentage of modal utterances in his study. The present study, however, only investigates the acquisition of Chinese modal verbs, without discussing other modal devices, such as main verbs, particles, modal adverbs, nouns and so on. Apart from different scopes of investigation, differences among English, French and Chinese, different caregiver input as well as individual differences between children may all contribute to the different percentages of modal utterances in total utterances.

2. Developmental Patterns of Modal Forms in the Child's Data Across Time Periods

Table 4-4 shows the developmental patterns of modal forms in the child's data across time periods. From Table 4-4, we can see that during period 2 modals 想 *xiǎng* 'desire' and 会 *huì* 'know how to' emerged, each accounting for 50% of all modal uses of period 2. During period 3, most target modal forms emerged, with four modals 想 *xiǎng* 'desire', 会 *huì* 'know how to', 要 *yào* 'want' and 能 *néng* 'can' taking up a large percentage of more than 70% of all modal uses of that period. These four modal forms continued to account for high percentages for the following periods, whereas modals 敢 *gǎn* 'dare', 用 *yòng* 'need to', 愿意 *yuànyi* 'willing', 可以 *kěyǐ* 'able to, may', 该 *gāi* 'should', 得 *děi* 'have to' and 喜欢 *xǐhuan* 'like' generally occurred with low frequency after their first occurrences. During period 8, modals 想 *xiǎng* 'desire', 会 *huì* 'know how to, may', 要 *yào* 'want, must' and 能 *néng* 'can' accounted for over 83% of all modal uses, while the remaining modals only accounted for 17%. Generally speaking, the most frequently occurring modal verb form was 要 *yào* 'want, must' (30.9%), followed by 想 *xiǎng* 'desire' (25.4%), 能 *néng* 'can' (17.3%) and 会 *huì* 'know how to, may' (10.1%). The least frequently occurring modal verb forms were 用 *yòng* 'need to' (0.4%) and 愿意 *yuànyì* 'willing' (0.4%).

Table 4-4   Distribution of modal forms in the child's data across time periods

	想 *xiǎng* %	会 *huì* %	要 *yào* %	敢 *gǎn* %	用 *yòng* %	愿意 *yuànyì* %	能 *néng* %	可以 *kěyǐ* %	该 *gāi* %	得 *děi* %	喜欢 *xǐhuan* %	Total %
P1	0	0	0	0	0	0	0	0	0	0	0	0
P2	50	50	0	0	0	0	0	0	0	0	0	100
P3	19	14.2	28.5	0	4.7	4.7	9.5	9.5	9.5	0	0	100
P4	7.8	13.1	42.1	10.5	0	0	15.7	0	10.5	0	0	100
P5	48.1	9.2	13.8	0.9	0.9	0.9	14.8	0.9	3.7	5.5	0.9	100
P6	14.4	6.3	45	0.9	0	0	18.9	0	0.9	13.5	0	100
P7	20	10	29	1	0	0	25	3	0	4	8	100
P8	23.8	8.9	37.3	7.4	0	0	13.4	2.9	0	5.9	0	100
Total	25.4	10.1	30.9	2.6	0.4	0.4	17.3	1.7	2.4	6.3	1.9	100

Some modals emerged early and occurred frequently, such as 想 *xiǎng* 'desire', 会 *huì* 'know how to, may' and 要 *yào* 'want, must', while some modals emerged late and occurred infrequently, such as 可以 *kěyǐ* 'able to, may', 该 *gāi* 'should' and 喜欢 *xǐhuān* 'like'. Some modals emerged early, but occurred with low frequency, such as 敢 *gǎn* 'dare', 用 *yòng* 'need to'and 愿意 *yuànyì* 'willing'. Some other modals emerged late, but occurred with high frequency, such as modal 能 *néng* 'can' which was the seventh emerged but the total frequency ranked the third among all modal uses, and modal 得 *děi* 'have to, must' which was the next to the last emerged but the total frequency ranked the fifth.

Erbaugh (1982: 607) notes that 要 *yào* 'want, must' was the most common modal in Pang's speech, accounting for 5% of all utterances, followed by 会 *huì* 'know how to, may' for 1.2%, and 可以 *kěyǐ* 'able to, may' for 0.4%. In Kang's speech, 要 *yào* 'want, must' was also the most common modal accounting for 0.5% in total utterances, and 会 *huì* 'know how to, may' accounted for 0.4%. Erbaugh mentions that 会 *huì* 'know how to, may' was the only modal productive in Pang's speech during 1; 10 to 2; 4, while she did not mention when modal 要 *yào* 'want, must' first emerged. Wells (1979) reports that modals *can* and *will* were the first two modals acquired as well as the two most frequently used modal verbs. The total frequencies of *can* and *will* ranked the third and the fifth respectively among all the auxiliary forms investigated. In the present study, modals 要 *yào* 'want, must' and 会 *huì* 'know how to, may' emerged early, and were also the most frequently occurring modals in the child's speech, taking up about 30% and 10% in total utterances respectively. It seems that some early acquired modals are also the ones most frequently used.

To sum up, the percentage of modal utterances in the child's data shows a steady trend of increase with the growth of the child. The lower percentages of modal utterances in the child's data, compared with the percentages of English modal utterances in previous researches, might be due to the different scopes of investigations, different caregiver input, as well as individual differences between children. There exist certain relation between the order of emergence of modals and the frequencies of occurrences of these modal forms in the child's data. Some modals emerged early and occurred frequently; while some emerged late and occurred infrequently. This relationship is not absolute, since there were also modal forms that emerged early but occurred infrequently, and modals that emerged lated but occurred frequently.

4.1.3 Summary

Chinese modal verbs emerged gradually between the end of 1; 8

and 2; 4, with most modals appearing before 2; 0. The first modal that emerged was in isolated use as an answer to an adult question, and most following modals that emerged were first used in spontaneous utterances. The first modal utterances were all simple declaratives with bare positive or negative modal forms. With the growth of the child, the percentages of modal utterances increased from 0 during period 1 to 7.1% during period 8. There exist certain relationship between the order of emergence and the percentage of uses for some modals.

4.2 The Acquisition of Semantics of Modals in the Child's Data

Research question 2 is answered by tracing the semantic categories of modals for their first appearance and the developmental pattern of the semantics of modals in the child's data across time periods.

4.2.1 The Semantic Category of Modals for the First Occurrence in the Child's Data

Figure 4-1 shows the semantic category of modals for the first occurrence. From the above figure, we can see that the first occurrences of modals were either dynamic modals or deontic modals. Modals 想 *xiǎng* 'desire', 会 *huì* 'know how to', 敢 *gǎn* 'dare', 愿意 *yuànyì* 'willing' and 喜欢 *xǐhuān* 'like' were dynamic modals for their first occurrence. Modals 要 *yào* 'must', 用 *yòng* 'need to', 能 *néng* 'can', 可以 *kěyǐ* 'may', 该 *gāi* 'should', 得 *děi* 'have to' were deontic modals for their first occurrence. The first occurrence of dynamic modal 想 *xiǎng* 'desire' was an answer to daddy's question, as is shown in example (1). The first occurrence of deontic modal 要 *yào* 'must' was a spontaneous utterance by the child, as is shown in example (2).

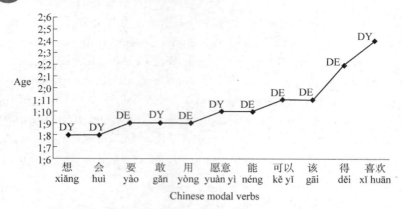

Figure 4-1   The semantic category of modals for the first occurrence in the child's data

(1) (The child was looking at a horse picture, and daddy asked
    her whether she wanted to ride a horse or not.) V 1; 8.27

    *FAT: 想   不   想   骑   马?

          Xiǎng   bù   xiǎng   qí   mǎ?

          want to not   want to ride   horse

          'Do you want to ride a horse?'

    *CHI: 想。

          Xiǎng.

          want to

          '(I) want to (ride a horse).'

    *FAT: 那   怎么   骑   马   呀?

          Nà   zěnme   qí   mǎ   ya?

          then   how   ride   horse   P

          'Then how to ride a horse?'

    *CHI: 0.[1]

    %act[2]: 在地上跳 (jump on the ground)

---

1 0 means the speaker says nothing.
2 % act represents the actions performed by the speaker.

(2) (The child wanted mommy to take her out while mommy was taking notes.) D 1; 9.13

妈妈	不	要	写。
māma	*bú*	*yào*	*xiě.*
mommy	not	must	write

'Mommy, do not write.'

In example (1), the child expressed her desire to ride a horse with a single modal form 想 *xiǎng* 'desire'. In example (2), the child expressed her prohibition on mommy's action with the negative form of deontic modal 要 *yào* 'must'. Examples of the first occurrence of each target modal forms are provided in the appendix 1.

Epistemic modal utterances first emerged around 2; 1. The following examples are the first epistemic modal utterances containing 该 *gāi* 'should', 要 *yào* 'must' and 会 *huì* 'may':

(3) (Qiān Qiān noticed her aunt took the umbrella and cup as she usually does before heading for the library) D 2; 0.31

姑姑	该	走	了。
Gūgu	gāi	zǒu	le.
aunt	should	leave	P

'Aunt should be leaving.'

(4) (Qiān Qiān saw her aunt standing on the edge of the bed tucking in the mosquito net) D 2; 1.19

姑姑	要	摔倒	了。
Gūgu	yào	shuāidǎo	le.
aunt	must	fall down	P

'Aunt will fall down.'

(5) (Grandma is fanning the child.) D 2; 1.29

白	扇住	脚	了,	会	疼	的。
Bái	shānzhù	jiǎo	le,	huì	téng	de.
don't	fan	foot	PHA	may	hurt	EMP

'Don't fan my foot, otherwise it may hurt.'

Epistemic modal utterances containing 该 *gāi* 'should' and 要 *yào* 'must' emerged earlier than those containing 会 *huì* 'may'. As has been discussed in chapter 2, 该 *gāi* 'should' and 要 *yào* 'must' express epistemic necessity, while 会 *huì* 'may' expresses epistemic possibility. It thus seems that modals denoting necessity were acquired earlier than those denoting possibility. The higher demand on the child's cognition imposed by epistemic possibility markers might have resulted in their later acquisition. It should be noted that only modal utterances containing epistemic 要 *yào* 'must' and 会 *huì* 'may' were captured by the audio and video recordings, while epistemic 该 *gāi* 'should' utterances were recorded only in the diary data.

The modal categories first emerged in the child's data were either dynamic or deontic modals. Epistemic modals emerged around 2; 1, with those expressing epistemic necessity emerging earlier than those expressing epistemic possibility.

4.2.2 Distribution of Semantic Categories of Modals in the Child's Data Across Time Periods

In this section, the developmental patterns of semantic categories of modals in the child's data across time periods are investigated. First, the distributional patterns of modal categories in the child's data across time periods are investigated. Second, the distributional patterns of semantic categories of modal forms in the child's data across time periods are investigated. Third, the semantics of modals in the child's data are investigated.

1. Distribution of Modal Categories in the Child's Data Across Time Periods

Figure 4-2 shows the evolution of dynamic, deontic and epistemic modals in the child's data. Dynamic modals emerged during period 2, followed by deontic modals emerging during period 3, and at last epistemic modals emerged during period 4. Generally speaking, dynamic modals were the most frequently occurring category of modals, taking up more than 70% of all modal uses, followed by deontic modals which took up over 24% of all modal uses, and epistemic modals occupied the lowest percentage of only 4%. The production of epistemic modals showed a steady trend of increase, while the relative frequencies of dynamic and deontic modals showed a trend of decrease with varying degrees.

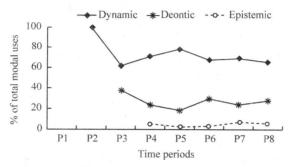

Figure 4-2   Distribution of modal categories in the child's data across time periods

As has been reviewed in chapter 2, most longitudinal studies on the acquisition of modal auxiliary verbs in different languages, including English, Modern Greek, German, Polish and French, converge on the finding that dynamic and deontic modals are acquired before epistemic modals (Wells 1979, 1985; Stephany 1986, 1993; Shatz & Wilcox 1991; Smoczyńska 1993; Bassano 1996; Papafragou 1998; Torr 1998). The developmental progression from dynamic and deontic modals to epistemic modals is consistent with the frequency data in language development, that is, dynamic and deontic modals are consistently more frequent than epistemic modals both in English and in French (Wells 1979; Bassano 1996; Torr 1998). The developmental and distributional patterns of modal categories observed in the present study generally speaking agree with those reported by previous studies.

Researchers propose different explanations for the late emergence of epistemic modals. Stephany (1986: 393) notes that as the linguistic forms serving to convey epistemic modality are of the same type as those used to express dynamic and deontic modality, and are to a large extent even identical with them, the reason for the later development of epistemically modalized utterances cannot be sought in linguistic complexity but must rather lie in cognitive complexity. Similar to Perkins (1983), Stephany also resorts to the cognitive developmental stages proposed by Piaget as the explanation framework for the later development of epistemic modals, which, however, does not accord with the age of acquisition of epistemic modals in naturalistic studies.

Some other researchers (Gopnik & Astington 1988; Papafragou 1998; Farrar & Maag 2002) propose that the late acquisition of epistemic modals is related to the development of theory of mind in children. Most three-year-olds fail false belief tasks, and only by 4; 0 or 5; 0 can children answer the questions in false-belief tasks correctly. This means that children of 4; 0 or 5; 0 realize that beliefs can be different from reality and that beliefs may be held with more or less certainty, which is a prerequisite for the acquisition of epistemic modals. That is why epistemic modals are rare before the third year, and mostly appear beyond 3; 6 years (Papafragou 2000: 164). Recall, however, that the findings of the studies on spontaneous speech indicate that children begin producing epistemic modals at around 2; 6. Thus, the theory of mind hypothesis shows a somewhat later development of epistemic modality than the findings of naturalistic data. The discrepancy is probably due to a certain degree of unnaturalness inherent in false belief tasks.

Besides cognitive complexity, it is also observed that caregiver input is partly related to the late emergence of epistemic modals

(Wells 1979; Shatz, Grimm and Wilcox 1990). The relation between caregiver input and modal acquisition will be discussed in detail in 4.5.

It is worth noting that Chinese epistemic modals 该 *gāi* 'should', 要 *yào* 'must' and 会 *huì* 'may' first emerged in the child's data about 2; 1, which is much earlier than the emergence of English epistemic modals around 2; 6. Why do Chinese epistemic modals emerge earlier than English epistemic modals?

Previous studies show that some aspects of epistemic meanings denoting epistemic necessity are within the capacity of children around 2;0, while the prototypical epistemic meanings denoting lower possibility usually emerge later. Through investigation on the use of epistemic modal terms *maybe, possibly, probably* and *might* among 10 children in the CHILDES database between ages 2;0 and 4;11, O'Neill and Atance (2000) discovers that English epistemic terms *maybe* and *probably* first appeared between 2; 0 and 2; 5. Choi (1991) discovers that Korean grammaticalized evidential sentence-ending suffixes were acquired between 1; 8 and 3; 0. Bassano (1996) discoveres that French lexicalized epistemic devices expressing prediction first emerged during 2; 1. All the above studies suggest that some aspects of epistemic notions may within the grasp of two-year-olds. The prototypical epistemic meanings denoting lower possibility, on the other hand, usually emerge later. According to O'Neill and Atance, epistemic modal *might* emerged after 2; 6 and started to be used frequently after 3; 6. Bassano notes that forms expressing the prototypical epistemic modal functions of belief and possibility utterances were not found before 2; 6. Chinese modals 该 *gāi* 'should' and 要 *yào* 'must' denote epistemic necessity, and therefore were acquired early by the child. Modal 会 *huì* 'may', which denotes high level of epistemic possibility, was acquired later than 该 *gāi* 'should' and 要 *yào* 'must'. The prototypical epistemic possibility marker 能 *néng* 'can' did not emerge until the child was 3; 3, which shows the low level of epistemic possibility meaning is beyond the grasp of the child until 3; 3.

To sum up, dynamic and deontic modals not only emerged earlier than epistemic modals, but also were more frequently occurring than epistemic modals. The later emergence of epistemic modals, as compared with dynamic and deontic modals, might be related to children's ability of theory of mind which presents great challenges for young children. The earlier emergence of Chinese epistemic modals, along with previous studies on the acquisition of Korean epistemic sentence-ending suffixes and French lexicalized epistemic modal makers, show that some epistemic notions may be within the grasp of children around 2; 0.

2. Distribution of Semantic Categories of Modal Forms in the Child's Data Across Time Periods

In this section, the distributional patterns of semantic categories of each modal form across time periods are described and discussed.

From Table 4-5, we can see the detailed semantic developmental patterns of modals in the child's data across time periods. Firstly, some uses of modals did not emerge in the child's data until she was 3; 3. For example, until period 8 the dynamic use of 用 *yòng* 'need to' as well as the epistemic use of 能 *néng* 'can' and 得 *děi* 'must' did not emerge[1].

Secondly, the distributional patterns of semantic categories of polysemous modals were different. Modals 会 *huì* 'know how to, may' and 要 *yào* 'want, must' were mainly used as dynamic modals, while 能 *néng* 'can', 可以 *kěyǐ* 'able to, may' and 得 *děi* 'have to, must' were

---

1 As has been mentioned earlier, 该 *gāi* was also used as an epistemic modal by the child according to diary data. Table 4-5 is based on audio and video transcriptions, which failed to capture the epistemic use of 该 *gāi*.

mainly used as deontic modals.

Thirdly, the semantic category first emerged was usually the dominant semantic category of modals (refer to Table 4-5 and Figure 4-1). For example, 会 *huì* 'know how to, may' was mainly used as a dynamic modal, and its dynamic use emerged first. 能 *néng* 'can', 可以 *kěyǐ* 'able to, may' and 得 *děi* 'have to, must' were mainly used as deontic modals, and their deontic use emerged first. The only exception to this pattern is 要 *yào* 'want, must', which was mainly used as a dynamic modal, but it was first used as a deontic modal.

Last but not least, the percentages of the semantic categories of each modal form across time periods were constantly changing, which shows that the development of the semantics of modals is a dynamic process.

Table 4-5   Distribution of the semantic categories of each modal form in the child's data across time periods

Modal forms	Modal categories	P1 %	P2 %	P3 %	P4 %	P5 %	P6 %	P7 %	P8 %	Total %
想 *xiǎng*	DY	0	100	100	100	100	100	100	100	100
会 *huì*	DY	0	100	100	80	70	57.1	30	66.7	65.2
	EP	0	0	0	20	30	42.9	70	33.3	34.8
要 *yào*	DY	0	0	66.7	93.8	86.7	90	79.3	56	80.9
	DE	0	0	33.3	0	13.3	10	20.7	36	17
	EP	0	0	0	6.2	0	0	0	8	2.1
敢 *gǎn*	DY	0	0	0	100	100	100	100	100	100
用 *yòng*	DY	0	0	0	0	0	0	0	0	0
	DE	0	0	100	0	100	0	0	0	100
愿意 *yuànyi*	DY	0	0	100	0	100	0	0	0	100
能 *néng*	DY	0	0	0	16.7	25	38.1	56	44.4	39.2
	DE	0	0	100	83.3	75	61.9	44	55.6	60.8
	EP	0	0	0	0	0	0	0	0	0
可以 *kěyǐ*	DY	0	0	50	0	100	0	0	50	37.5
	DE	0	0	50	0	0	0	100	50	62.5
该 *gāi*	DE	0	0	100	100	100	100	0	0	100
	EP	0	0	0	0	0	0	0	0	0
得 *děi*	DY	0	0	0	0	83.3	6.7	0	0	20.7
	DE	0	0	0	0	16.7	93.3	100	100	79.3
	EP	0	0	0	0	0	0	0	0	0
喜欢 *xǐhuan*	DY	0	0	0	0	100	0	100	0	100

Dynamic, deontic and epistemic modality can be realized in different modal forms. Are these modal forms equally frequent in expressing certain modal category? If not, which modal forms are more frequently used? Which modal forms are less frequently used? The percentages of each modal form in expressing dynamic, deontic and epistemic modalities are presented in Table 4-6.

As is shown in Table 4-6, each modal category was prevalent with certain modal forms, with other forms accounting for very low percentages. When used as dynamic modals, 想 *xiǎng* 'desire' and 要 *yào* 'want' were the most frequently occurring modal forms, accounting for 71% of all dynamic modal uses. 会 *huì* 'know how to' and 能 *néng* 'can' were used with some frequency, taking up about 20% of all dynamic modal uses. The remaining 6 modals altogether accounted for about 9% of dynamic modal uses.

Table 4-6 Distribution of the semantic categories of each modal form in the child's data

	DY (%)	DE (%)	EP (%)
想 *xiǎng*	35.9	×	×
会 *huì*	9.3	×	84.2
要 *yào*	35.3	21.2	15.8
敢 *gǎn*	3.7	×	×
用 *yòng*	0	1.8	×
愿意 *yuànyì*	0.6	×	×
能 *néng*	9.6	42.5	0
可以 *kěyǐ*	0.9	4.4	×
该 *gāi*	×	9.7	0
得 *děi*	1.9	20.4	0
喜欢 *xǐhuan*	2.8	×	×
Total	100	100	100

Notes: × represents non-existence of the modal category. 0 represents the child did not produce modals of the modal category.

When used as a deontic modal, 能 *néng* 'can' was the most

frequently occurring modal form, taking up 42.5% of all deontic modal uses, followed by deontic modals 要 *yào* 'must' and 得 *děi* 'have to' which accounting for about 20% each. Deontic modals 该 *gāi* 'should', 可以 *kěyǐ* 'may' and 用 *yòng* 'need to' altogether accounted for less than 16%.

会 *huì* 'may' and 要 *yào* 'must' were used to express epistemic modal meaning. Epistemic modal 会 *huì* 'may' took up a huge percentage of over 84%. In sharp contrast to the high frequency of 会 *huì* 'may', epistemic modal 要 *yào* 'must' only occupied about 16% of all epistemic modal uses.

The above discussion shows that the distributional patterns of the semantic categories of each modal form were different: some modals were mainly used as dynamic modals, whereas some were mainly used as deontic modals. Besides, the percentages of occurrences of each modal form in different modal categories are different: certain modal forms accounted for most uses of each semantic category.

3. Semantic Features of Chinese Modals in the Child's Data

In this section, the semantic features of Chinese modals in the child's data are investigated in terms of the three semantic categories of modality: dynamic, deontic and epistemic modals respectively. The pragmatic uses of modals, such as the use of 能 *néng* 'can' in rhetorical question to express dissatisfaction etc., were non-existent in the child's speech, and therefore only the semantics features are discussed here.

1) *The Semantic Features of Dynamic Modals in the Child's Data*

As has been discussed in chapter 2, dynamic modals 想 *xiǎng* 'desire', 要 *yào* 'want', 喜欢 *xǐhuan* 'like', 愿意 *yuànyì* 'willing' and 敢 *gǎn* 'dare' express the notion of desire; dynamic modals 会 *huì* 'know how to', 能 *néng* 'can' and 可以 *kěyǐ* 'able to' express the notion of ability; and dynamic modals 用 *yòng* 'need to' and 得 *děi* 'have to' express the notion of need. The semantics of these dynamic modals in the child's data are discussed here in detail.

想 *xiǎng* 'desire', 要 *yào* 'want', 喜欢 *xǐhuan* 'like', 愿意 *yuànyì* 'willing'& 敢 *gǎn* 'dare'

Dynamic modals 想 *xiǎng* 'desire' and 要 *yào* 'want' each accounted for over 35% of all dynamic modal uses in the child's data, while 喜欢 *xǐhuan* 'like', 愿意 *yuànyì* 'willing' and 敢 *gǎn* 'dare' altogether took up over 7% of all dynamic modal uses.

Modal 想 *xiǎng* 'desire' can only be used as a dynamic modal expressing weak desire. Most (60%) dynamic modal 想 *xiǎng* 'desire' utterances were about the child's desire (6), and some (37%) utterances were about other's desire (7).

(6) (The child touches mommy's bag which has jelly in it.) D 2; 1.24

芊芊	想	拿住	(果冻)。
Qiān Qian	*xiǎng*	*názhu*	*(guǒdòng).*
Qian Qian	desire	hold	(jelly)

'Qian Qian wants to hold (the jelly).'

(7) (The child is playing house with a doll.) V 2; 5.18

小妹妹	她	她	想	坐	哩。
Xiǎomèimei	*tā*	*tā*	*xiǎng*	*zuò*	*li.*
little sister	she	she	desire	sit	P.

'The little sister wants to sit.'

Most dynamic modal 要 *yào* 'want' utterances were mainly (67%) used to express the child's strong desire (8), or sometimes (30%) other's strong desire (9).

(8) (In the morning, the child asks to change her clothes and go out. Mommy tells her to have her breakfast first. The child disobeys mommy and walks into the bedroom to change her

clothes.) D 2; 11.18

我	就	要		换!
Wǒ	jiù	yào		huàn!
I	EMP	want to		change

'I WANT to change (my clothes)!'

(9) (The child plays house with the doll. The child complains the doll wouldn't sit well.) V 2; 4.04

她	非得	要	歪。
Tā	fēiděi	yào	wāi.
she	EMP	want to	askew

'She just want to sit askew.'

喜欢 xǐhuan 'like' can only be used as a dynamic modal, expressing a sense of enjoyment of doing something. The child mainly (89%) used 喜欢 xǐhuan 'like' to express a strong personal preference for certain things or actions (10).

(10) (The child wants to wear mommy's high-heel shoes. Mommy forbids her to do that.) D 2; 6.18

我	喜欢	穿	你的	高跟鞋。
Wǒ	xǐhuan	chuān	nǐde	gāogēnxié.
I	like	wear	your	high-heel shoes.

'I like to wear your high-heel shoes.'

Like modals 想 xiǎng 'desire' and 喜欢 xǐhuan 'like', 愿意 yuànyì 'willing' can only be used as a dynamic modal. Unlike modals 想 xiǎng 'desire' and 喜欢 xǐhuan 'like' which represented an active force on the part of the actor to actualize an action, dynamic modal 愿意 yuànyì 'willing' represented a passive resistance on the part of the actor to an external force (11).

(11) (The child tells daddy she wants to sit on an elephant.) D 1; 11.29

愿意	让	芊芊	坐。

> *Yuànyi   ràng   Qiān Qian   zuò.*
> willing   let   Qian Qian   sit
> '(The elephant) is willing to let Qian Qian sit on it.'

Most (83%) 敢 *gǎn* 'dare' utterances were used to express the child's courage to do something (12).

(12) (Some kids are watching a spider on the ground. One of them askes Qian Qian whether she is afraid of the spider or not.) V 3; 2.09

我　敢　踩　蜘蛛,　我　不　怕。

Wǒ   gǎn   cǎi   zhīzhū,   wǒ   bú   pà.

'I dare to stamp on the spider, and I am not afraid (of it).'

会 *huì* 'know how to', 能 *néng* 'can' & 可以 *kěyǐ* 'able to'

Dynamic modals 会 *huì* 'know how to' and 能 *néng* 'can' each account for over 9% of all dynamic modal uses in the child's data, while 可以 *kěyǐ* 'able to' only takes up less than 1%.

Most (59%) dynamic 会 *huì* 'know how to' utterances were used to express the acquisition of specific skills by the child herself (13).

(13) (The child successes in taking off her clothes.) D 2; 0.26

芊芊　　会　　　　　脱　　　了.

Qiān Qian   huì   　　　tuō   le.

Qian Qian   know how to   　　take off   PHA

'Qian Qian knows how to take off (clothes).'

Most (69%) dynamic modal 能 *néng* 'can' utterances indicated the child's possession of certain power (14).

(14) (The child has been walking with her aunt for a while. Her aunt offers to hold her.)   D 2; 0.26

我　能　　跑。

Wǒ   néng   pǎo.

I   can   run

'I can run.'

Most (67%) dynamic modal 可以 *kěyǐ* 'able to' utterances denoted the possession of certain power by the child on condition that something else had happened (15).

(15) (The child asks daddy to buy a motorbike. Daddy asks her why.) D 2; 1.10

我　可以　坐　　了。

Wǒ kěyǐ zuò le.

I　can　sit　PHA

'I can sit on it.'

用 *yòng* 'need to' & 得 *děi* 'have to'

Modal 用 *yòng* 'need to' can be used as a dynamic modal as well as a deontic modal, while in the child's data the dynamic use of modal 用 *yòng* 'need to' does not exist.

As a dynamic modal, 得 *děi* 'have to' referred to constraining forces internal to the child, like hunger, thirst, exhaustion, excretion (16).

(16) (The child poops for the second time during the day. Mommy asks her why she poops again.) D 3; 2.29

因为　肚子里有　　虫虫。　　大人　得　拉　　一　　次,

Yīnwéi dùzi lǐ yǒu chóngchong. Dàrén děi lā yí cì,

because belly inside have worm, adults need poop one CL

小孩　　得　　拉　　两　　次。

xiǎohái děi lā liǎng cì.

Kids　　need　poop　two　CL.

'(I poop again) because I have worms in my belly. Adults need to poop once (a day), while kids need to poop twice (a day).'

2) The Semantic Features of Deontic Modals in the Child's Data

As has been discussed in chapter 2, deontic modals 要 *yào* 'must', 该 *gāi* 'should' and 得 *děi* 'must' express the notion of obligation; deontic modals 能 *néng* 'can' and 可以 *kěyǐ* 'may' express the notion of permission; deontic modal 用 *yòng* 'need to' expresses the notion of necessity. The semantics of these deontic modals in the child's data are discussed here in detail.

要 *yào* 'must', 该 *gāi* 'should' & 得 *děi* 'have to'

Deontic modal 要 *yào* 'must' and 得 *děi* 'have to' each accounted for over 20% of all modal uses, while deontic modal 该 *gāi* 'should' occupied less than 10%.

As a deontic modal, 要 *yào* 'must' utterances in the child's data were mainly (63%) used in the negative form 不要 *bú yào* 'not must', expressing the child's prohibition on other's action (17).

(17) (The child's aunt kicked her toy goose by accident.) D 2; 0.16

不	要	踢	我	鹅。
Bú	*yào*	*tī*	*wǒ*	*é.*
not	must	kick	my	goose.

'Do not kick my goose.'

As a deontic modal, 该 *gāi* 'should' was most (82%) often used to express actions that is about to occur based on routine (18).

(18) (The child has been brushing her teeth for a while, and then she asks grandma whether it's time to gargle or not.) D 2; 4.21

该	漱口	了	吧?
Gāi	*shùkǒu*	*le*	*ba?*
should	gargle	PHA	P

'Should I gargle or not?'

All the deontic modal 得 *děi* 'have to' appeared in its positive modal form, indicating a neutral or sometimes negative attitude with respect to the child's desire (19).

(19) (The child is dancing naked in front of the mirror.) D 3; 0.22

不　　能　　光　　屁股　　跳舞，我　得　穿　　上　　　裤头。

Bù　néng　guāng pìgǔ　tiàowǔ, wǒ　děi　chuān shàng　kùtóu.

not　can　　naked ass　　dance, I have to put on　underwear

'I can not dance naked, and I have to put on my underwear.'

能 *néng* 'can' & 可以 *kěyǐ* 'may'

Deontic modal 能 *néng* 'can' was the most frequently occurring deontic modal form (42.5%). In contrast to the high frequency of 能 *néng* 'can', 可以 *kěyǐ* 'may' which also expresses permission, was only used for 4.4% among all the deontic modal utterances.

Deontic modal 能 *néng* 'can' mainly (67%) appeared in its negative form 不能 *bù néng* 'can not', expressing the child's prohibition on other's action (20).

(20) (The child is making the handwork.) A 2; 8.13

谁　　　　也　　　不　能　　　捣乱!

Shuí　　yě　　bù　néng　　dǎoluàn!

anyone　EMP　not　can　　make trouble

'No one can make trouble.'

Deontic modal 可以 *kěyǐ* 'may' utterances mainly (80%) appeared in its positive form, expressing the child's permission to other's action (21):

(21) (The child pretends to go to work. Mommy asks to follow her to the workplace.) D 2; 6.07

你　也　可以　　跟着　　我。

Nǐ　yě　kěyǐ　　gēnzhe　wǒ.

you also　may　　follow　me

'You may also follow me.'

用 *yòng* 'need'

Most (94%) the deontic modal 用 *yòng* 'need' were in the negative form 不用 *bú yòng* 'not need', canceling other's actions (22).

(22) (Mommy showers the child and rubs her arms.) D 2; 1.10

不	用	搓	胳膊。
Bú	*yòng*	*cuō*	*gēbo.*
not	need	rub	arm

'You do not need to rub my arms.'

3) The Semantic Features of Epistemic Modals in the Child's Data

Only two modal forms were used to express epistemic modal notions: 会 *huì* 'may' and 要 *yào* 'must', with 会 *huì* 'may' accounting for 84% of all epistemic modal uses and 要 *yào* 'must' accounting for the remaining 16%.

Most (74%) epistemic modal 会 *huì* 'may' occurred in its positive form, expressing the child's estimation on the possibility of certain occurrences (23).

(23) (The child is playing house with a toy duck. She let the duck drink water from a plate.) V 2; 8.27

呛住	就	会 难受,	吃药	打针	xx xx.
Qiàngzhu	*jiù*	*huì nánshòu,*	*chīyào*	*dǎzhēn*	*xx xx.*
choke	EMP	may feel bad,	have medicine	take an injection	

'(If the duck) is choked, (it) will feel bad, and (have to) have medicine and take an injection.'

Epistemic modal 要 *yào* 'must' appeared only in its positive modal form, expressing the child's prediction on future occurrences (24).

(24) (The child's aunt is standing on the edge of the bed, tucking in the mosquito net.) D 2; 1.19

姑姑	要	摔	倒	了.

Gūgu   yào   shuāi   dǎo   le.
aunt   must fall   down   PHA.
'Aunt is going to fall down.'

The above discussion shows that the uses of modal forms in the same semantic category illustrated similar as well as different features.

4.2.3   Summary

Generally speaking, the developmental pattern of Chinese modals progressed from dynamic and deontic modals to epistemic modals. This developmental pattern was consistent with the frequency data of modal uses. Dynamic modals were the most frequent category of modality, accounting for over 70% of all modal uses, followed by deontic modals for 24%, and epistemic modals accounted for the lowest frequency of over 4%. The late emergence of epistemic modals may be related to their cognitive complexity and less caregiver input.

The distributional patterns of semantic categories of modals are different: some modals were mainly used as dynamic modals, while some others were mainly used as deontic modals. The semantic category of the first occurrence of each modal was always the dominant semantic category of that modal. The distribution of the three semantic categories of modals across time periods was a dynamic process toward the adult use. Until the end of the investigation, some uses of modals did not emerge, which shows modal acquisition lasts to later period in child development. The percentages of use of different modal forms of each semantic category are different: dynamic modality was mainly realized in the forms of modals 想 *xiǎng* 'desire' and 要 *yào* 'want'; deontic modality was mainly realized in the forms of 能 *néng* 'can', 要 *yào* 'must' and 得 *děi* 'have to'; and epistemic modals was mainly realized in the form of 会

huì 'may'.

The investigation into the semantic characterizations of modal uses in the child's data shows that generally speaking the child could select appropriate modals for given speech situations. Dynamic modals were mainly used by the child to express her own abilities, desires and intentions. Deontic modals were mainly used to express the child's permission or prohibition on other's actions. Epistemic modals were mainly used to express the child's estimation on the possibility or probability of future occurrences.

4.3 The Acquisition of Syntactic Structures of Modal Utterances in the Child's Data

Research question 3 is answered by investigating the early syntactic structures and later syntactic development of modal utterances.

4.3.1 Distribution of Syntactic Structures of Modal Utterances in the Child's Data Across Time Periods

This section first examines the features of early syntactic structures of modal utterances, and then the developmental patterns of later modal utterances in the child's data.

1. Early Syntactic Structures of Modal Utterances in the Child's Data

After examining the syntactic structures of early modal utterances (the first five occurrences of modals in appendix 1), we have discovered the following developmental patterns.

Firstly, early modal utterances developed from declaratives to questions, with declaratives accounting for the great majority of these early modal utterances. Modals were only used in declaratives until the child was 2; 0.20, when she produced her first interrogative modal utterance 拿这个可以吧 *ná zhège kěyǐ ba* 'can (I) hold this'. There were altogether 3 interrogatives among the first modal utterances. The first five utterances of semantic categories of each modal form are provided in appendix 1.

Secondly, the structures of early modal utterances developed from simple bare modal forms to complete sentences. All the first five instances of dynamic 想 *xiǎng* 'desire' utterances were in the bare modal form 想 *xiǎng* 'desire' or 不想 *bù xiǎng* 'not desire'. Three of the first five dynamic 会 *huì* 'know how to' utterances were in its bare positive form 会 *huì* 'know how to', and the other two developed to more complex structures, as in 爸爸会 *bàba huì* 'daddy can', and 爸爸会写字 *bàba huì xiězì* 'daddy can write'. The syntactic structures of the following modal utterances developed to complete sentences with subject, verb and object, as in 妈妈不能吃蛋糕 *māma bù néng chī dàngāo* 'mommy can not have cake', 我喜欢穿你的高跟鞋 *wǒ xǐhuān chuān nǐde gāogēnxié* 'I like to wear your high-heel shoes', etc. The developmental pattern from bare modal forms in early modal utterances to complete sentences in later modal utterances suggests that the syntactic structures of early modal utterances facilitate the development of syntactic structures of later modal utterances.

The above discussion shows that early modal utterances developed from declaratives to interrogatives, and the structures of those utterances developed from simple bare modal forms to complete sentences. In the following section, the development of syntactic structures of later modal utterances in the child's data is investigated.

2. Later Syntactic Development of Modal Utterances in the Child's Data

Through investigation into the later syntactic development of modal utterances in the child's data, it is observed that those structures gradually became more and more diverse as the child grew up, which is represented by the diversification of sentence types, subjects, verbs and objects.

Firstly, as has been shown above, most early modal utterances were simple declaratives. Different types of interrogative constructions started to emerge with the child's growth.

As is shown in Table 4-7, the interrogative modal construction was first observed at 2; 0 in the form of 可以 *kěyǐ* 'may' with the sentence final particle 吧 *ba* (25). Interrogative modal constructions were observed for most modals, with the exception of modals 愿意 *yuànyì* 'willing', 用 *yòng* 'need to', 得 *děi* 'have to, must', and certain semantic categories of 要 *yào* 'want, must', 能 *néng* 'can', 可以 *kěyǐ* 'able to, may' and 该 *gāi* 'should'.

Table 4-7   Age of the first occurrence of interrogative constructions in the child's data

	想 xiǎng	会 huì	要 yào	敢 gǎn	用 yòng	愿意 yuànyì	能 néng	可以 kěyǐ	该 gāi	得 děi	喜欢 xǐhuan
DY	D2;1.11	D2;3.23	D2;6.28	D2;7.26	0	0	D2;6.30	0	×	0	V2;10.01
DE	×	×	0	×	0	×	V2;3.05	D2;0.02	0	0	×
EP	D2;4.28	×	0	×	×	×	0	×	D2;4.21	0	×

Notes: × represents non-existence of the modal category. 0 represents non-existence of the modal utterance in the child's data

(25) (The child has taken mommy's CD box. Mommy forbids her from doing that. She then takes away mommy's notebook.) D 2; 0.20

拿　这个　可以　吧?
Ná　zhège　kěyǐ　ba?
take　this　may　P
'Can I take this?'

Interrogative modal constructions were found in various forms, such as [Modal+V+ 吧 / 吗 *ba/ma* 'particle'?] (25), [Modal+ 不 *bù* 'not'+Modal+V?] (26), [Modal+V?] in a rising intonation (27),

[Modal+V+干啥/干什么 *gàn shá/gàn shénme* 'do what'?] (28), or [为什么/咋 *wèishénme/zǎ* 'why' + Modal+V?] (29). Interrogatives accounted for 7.6% of all modal utterances in the child's data, and there was a marked increase of interrogatives since the child was 2; 8.

(26) (The child points to one of her shoes and asks mommy whether the shoe can make a sound or not.) D 2; 1.11

这个	会	不	会	响?
Zhège	*huì*	*bú*	*huì*	*xiǎng?*
this	can	not	can	make a sound

'Can this make a sound?'

(27) (Mommy is trying to put on the child's shoes.) D 2; 1.16

妈妈	不	会	穿?
Māma	*bú*	*huì*	*chuān?*
mommy	not	know how to	put on

'Doesn't mommy know how to put on (my shoes)?'

(28) (The child saw daddy was climbing down the ladder.) D 2; 6.27

你	要	下来	干啥?
Nǐ	*yào*	*xiàlái*	*gànshá?*
you	want	climb down	do what

'Why do you climb down?'

(29) (Mommy lay down on grandpa's bed to take a rest.) D 2; 6.28

妈妈	为什么	要	躺	姥爷	床?
Māma	*wèishénme*	*yào*	*tǎng*	*lǎoye*	*chuáng?*
mommy	why	want	lie down on	grandpa	bed

'Why does mommy lie down on grandpa's bed?'

Secondly, the structures of subjects of modal utterances became more diverse gradually. As has been discussed earlier, the first modal utterances were in the bare positive or negative modal forms without subjects. Later modal utterances started to include increasingly complex subjects. The child first used her own name 芊芊 *Qiān Qiān* to refer to herself since 1; 11, and then she started to use first person pronoun 我 *wǒ* 'I' since 2; 1. 我 *wǒ* 'I' was used frequently since 2; 3 and gradually replaced 芊芊 *Qiān Qiān*. The child first used nouns, such as 妈妈 *māma* 'mommy', 爸爸 *bàba* 'daddy', 婆婆 *pópo* 'grandma', etc., as second and third person referents. Second personal pronoun 你 *nǐ* 'you' emerged during 2; 6, started to be used frequently since 2; 8 and gradually replaced nouns as the second person referent. Third personal pronoun 他/她/它 *tā* 'he/she/it, him/her/it' emerged during 2; 2, started to be used frequently since 2; 4, and gradually replaced nouns as the third person referent. Phrases emerged since 2; 1, and started to be used frequently since 2; 4, as in (30). Clauses emerged since 2; 5, and were used frequently since 2; 7, as in (31):

(30) (The child is chewing bubble gum.) D 2; 5.13

吃	很	多	会	坏	牙。
Chī	*hěn*	*duō*	*huì*	*huài*	*yá.*
eat	very	many	may	harm	teeth

'Eating lots of (candy) may do harm to the teeth.'

(31) (The child is drinking soup.) D 2; 9.21

妈妈	你	要是	渴	时候	能	喝	这个	汤。
māma	*nǐ*	*yàoshi*	*kě*	*shíhòu*	*néng*	*hē*	*zhège*	*tāng.*
mommy	you	if	thirsty	time	can	drink	this	soup

'Mommy, when you are thirsty you can drink this soup.'

Thirdly, the structures of verbs of modal utterances became more diverse gradually. The first modal utterances were in the bare positive or negative modal forms. Later modal utterances started to include increasingly complex verbs. Modal forms developed from bare positive or negative forms to complex structures. For example, the [Mod+不 *bù* 'not' + Mod] structure first emerged at 2; 0 in the form of 可不可以 *kě bù kěyǐ* 'may not may' (32), and then started to be used frequently since 2; 4. Besides the diversification of modal forms, adverbs started to appear in front of modals since 2; 2. The first adverb appeared in front of modals was adverb of manner 还 *hái* 'still', as in (33), and then different kinds of adverbs started to be used frequently since 2; 4, such as adverb of degree 好 *hǎo* 'very', adverb of scope 只 *zhǐ* 'only' and 都 *dōu* 'all', adverb of time 原来 *yuánlái* 'formerly', 刚才 *gāngcái* 'just now' and 现在 *xiànzài* 'now', adverb of manner 还 *hái* 'still' and 也 *yě* 'also', and so on. The structures after modals developed from simple high frequency verbs, such as 喝 *hē* 'drink', 走 *zǒu* 'walk', 吃 *chī* 'eat', etc., to complex verbs, adjectives and even clauses, such as 抛弃 *pāoqì* 'abandon', 小心 *xiǎoxīn* 'careful', 把字句 *bǎzìjù* 'bǎ clause' (34), etc.

(32) (Grandpa is shelling shrimps for the child.) D 2; 0.03

芊芊		剥	可	不	可以?
Qiān Qian	bō	kě	bù	kěyǐ?
Qian Qian	shell	may	not	may

'May I shell (shrimps)?'

(33) (The child pretends to cry.) D 2; 2.01

我	还	想	哭.
Wǒ	hái	xiǎng	kū.
I	still	want	cry

'I still want to cry.'

(34) (Grandpa climbs up stairs holding Qian Qian's hand in case she might fall down.) D 2; 5.07

这个楼	好	高	会	把	你	摔	下来。
Zhègelóu	hǎo	gāo	huì	bǎ	nǐ	shuāi	xiàlái.
this building	very	tall	may	Executive Marker	you	fall down

'This building is very tall, and you might fall down.'

Fourthly, the structures of objects of modal utterances became more diverse gradually. The first modal utterances were in the bare positive or negative modal forms without object. Later modal utterances started to include increasingly complex objects. Phrases emerged since 2; 1 (35), started to become more frequent and complex since 2; 4 (36).

(35) (Grandpa caught a cicada for the child) D 2; 1.06

蚂妞	不	会	吃	我的	面包。
Māniū	*bú*	*huì*	*chī*	*wǒde*	*miànbāo.*
cicada	not	can	eat	my	bread

'The cicada can not eat my bread.'

(36) (Grandpa starts to have his dinner in the kitchen while the child is playing by herself in bedroom) D 2; 4.04

我	要	去	看看	姥爷	吃	饭。
Wǒ	*yào*	*qù*	*kànkan*	*lǎoye*	*chī*	*fàn.*
I	want	go	look at	grandpa	eat	meal

'I want to go to take a look at grandpa while he is having his dinner.'

The above analysis shows that the syntactic structures of modal utterances in the child's data developed from simple constructions to complex constructions gradually, which was exemplified by the diversification of sentence types and the syntactic structures of subjects, verbs and objects respectively.

Both Fletcher (1978) and Shatz, Billman and Yaniv (1986) note that declaratives appear earlier and are much more frequent than questions in the modal utterances produced by their subjects. The two researchers differ, however, as to whether the sentence types develop quickly during the early period of modal acquisition. Fletcher's data show that two in five modal forms appeared in at least two kinds of sentence types, while Shatz et al.'s data show that more than 83% of all modal forms only appeared in declaratives. The present study finds that declaratives emerged earlier than questions in Chinese modal acquisition, and declaratives accounted for almost 93% of all modal utterances, which agree with the earlier emergence and the predominance of declaratives in modal utterances as reported by previous researchers. The present study also shows that eight of the eleven modal forms appeared both in declaratives and in various question forms, which suggests that sentence types of modal utterances developed quickly as revealed by Fletcher's study.

Investigations into the development of subjects, verbs, and objects of modal utterances by different researchers have come to different conclusions. Diessel (cited in Tomasello 2003: 246-248) asserts that children first used concatenatives in very formulaic ways: *I wanna/ hafta/gonna verb phrase*, and then these formulaic constructions gradually developed to diverse constructions. Fletcher's (1978) data, on the other hand, reveal that the first modal utterances were not formulaic at all, and rather the structures of early modal utterances developed quickly from simple constructions to complex constructions. Through detailed investigation into the development of syntactic structures of subjects, verbs, and objects of modal utterances, the present study shows that the first modal utterances were simple but not formulaic, and modal utterances developed gradually from simple constructions to complex constructions. The differences of early syntactic structures might be related to different acquisition styles by children, as well as different conversation styles by caregivers.

To sum up, the syntactic structures of later modal utterances developed from simple constructions to complex constructions, which disagrees with the findings of Dissel that modal utterances developed from formulaic constructions to diverse constructions.

4.3.2   Sentence Types and Semantic Categories of Modals in the Child's Data

In this section, the relationsip between sentence types and semantic categories of modals in the child's data is investigated.

From Table 4-8, we can see the following patterns. Firstly, most modals in the child's data were in affirmatives, while only a few were in interrogatives. Secondly, deontic modals were more likely to occur in negatives compared with dynamic and epistemic modals.

Table 4-8   Sentence types and modal categories in the child's data

Modal semantic categories	Affirmative (%)	Sentence types Negative (%)	Interrogative (%)	Total(%)
DY	76.3	15.6	8.1	100
DE	53	41.7	5.3	100
EP	89.5	10.5	0	100

Pea and Mawby (1984) report that most of the modals were used in the affirmative sentences and negative modals were used only to express constraints on action or an unwillingness to act at the time of speaking. Results of the present study agree with those in Pea and Mawby's study. Why are affirmative modal utterances prevalent in children's speech? Why are interrogative modal utterances rarely used? As has been discussed earlier, declarative modal utterances appeared earlier than interrogative modal utterances in the acquisition process, which suggests that declaratives may be linguistically simpler as well as less cognitive-demanding than interrogatives. These factors, together with the effect of caregiver input (to be discussed in detail in 4.5), might have resulted in the prevalence of affirmatives.

4.3.3 Subjecthood and Semantic Categories of Modals in the Child's Data

In this section, the relationship between subjecthood and modal categories in the child's data is investigated.

Table 4-9   Subjecthood and modal categories in the child's data

Modal semantic categories	Self (%)	Subjecthood Others (%)	Neither (%)	Total(%)
DY	64.9	30.1	5	100
DE	29.8	57.9	12.3	100
EP	26.3	52.6	21.1	100

Subjects referring to self were realized in the form of null subject (e.g. 要屙屎 *yào ē shǐ* '(I) wanna poop'), the child's nickname 芊芊 *Qiān Qian*, or the first personal pronoun 我 *wǒ* 'I'. Subjects referring to others were realized in the form of null subject (e.g. 不要跑 *bú yào pǎo* '(Little worm) do not run away'), forms of address to others (e.g. 妈妈 *māma* 'mommy', 爸爸 *bàba* 'daddy', 婆婆 *pópo* 'grandpa', etc.), the second personal pronoun 你 *nǐ* 'you', or the third personal pronoun 他/她 *tā* 'it/he/she'. Subjects referring to neither were realized in the form of null subjects (e.g. 要下雨了 *yào xiàyǔ le* '(It's) going to rain'), names of animals (e.g. 小鸽子 *xiǎo gēzi* 'little pidgeon'), and demonstrative pronouns (e.g. 这个 *zhège* 'this').

From Table 4-9, we can see the following patterns. Firstly, most dynamic modal utterances had subjects referring to the child herself, which suggests that most dynamic modal utterances expressed the child's abilities, intentions and desires, for example, 我能够着了 *wǒ néng gòuzháo le* 'I can reach it'. Secondly, most deontic modal utterances had subjects referring to others, which suggests that most deontic modal utterances expressed the child's prohibition on others' actions, for example, 姐姐不能坐 *jiějie bù néng zuò* 'The sister can not sit'. Thirdly, most epistemic modal utterances had subjects referring to others, which suggests that most epistemic modal utterances expressed the child's estimation on the probability of other's intentions, such as 安安会打我吗 *An An huì dǎ wǒ ma* 'may An An beat me'.

Pea and Mawby (1984) also notes there seems to be a relation between specific type of modality and subjecthood. They examined the semantics of modal auxiliary verbs (*can, will, gonna*) in six children aged between 2; 4 and 2; 10, and found that children used dynamic modals with first person pronoun *I* to express volition of the self 80% to 95% of the time (e.g. *I will give you a tiny little fork*). The present study also reveals similar findings with respect to the relationship between dynamic modals and the first person referents. Why do dynamic modal utterances tend to have subjects referring to self in children's speech? It seems that children's development from egocentrism to decentration might be the reason for the prevalence of first person referents in dynamic modal utterances. Piaget claims that young children are egocentric. This does not mean that they are selfish, but that they see things from their own point of view. As children grow older, they become capable of de-centering [1] and could appreciate viewpoints other than their own. In other words, they were capable of cognitive perspective-taking. That is why young children tend to express the abilities, desires and intentions of their own instead of those of others.

4.3.4 Summary

The syntactic structures of modal utterances in the child's data developed from simple constructions to complex constructions gradually with the diversification of sentence types as well as the constructions of subjects, verbs and objects of modal utterances. There existed certain relationship between sentence types and modal categories in the child's data. Most modals appeared in affirmative sentences, while only a few in interrogative sentences. Negatives were most frequently occurring in deontic modal utterances. Linguistic factors as well as cognitive development might be responsible for the distributional pattern. Apart from the relation between sentence types and modal categories, there also existed certain relationship between subjecthood and modal categories. Most dynamic modal utterances had subjects referring to the child herself; most deontic modal utterances had subjects referring to others; most epistemic modal utterances had subjects referring to others. Children's cognitive development from egocentrism to decentration has been proposed as

---

1 According to Piaget (1965: 264), de-centering means the ability to become aware of others' points of view.

a possible explanation for the prevalence of first person subjects in dynamic modal utterances.

4.4   A Comparison of the Features of Modals in the Caregivers' Data and in the Child's Data Across Time Periods

Research question 4 is answered by investigating the formal, semantic and syntactic features of modals in the caregivers' data across time periods, and then comparing these features with corresponding features in the child's data.

4.4.1   Distribution of Modal Forms in the Caregivers' Data and in the Child's Data Across Time Periods

In this section, the distributional and developmental patterns of modal utterances and modal forms in the caregivers' data are investigated, which are further compared with those features in the chid's data.

1. Distribution of Modal Utterances in the Caregivers' Data and in the Child's Data Across Time Periods

Table 4-10 presents the distribution of modal utterances in the caregivers' data across time periods. From the above table, we can see that there are 1478 modal utterances in the caregivers' data, which represented over 6% of the total sampled utterances. The percentage of modal utterances was over 5% during period 1, which dropped to nearly 4% during period 2, and then the percentage showed a general trend of steady rise to over 11% during period 8.

The distributional patterns of modal utterances in the caregivers' data and in the child's data across time periods were compared in Figure 4-3. As is shown in the figure, the distribution of modal utterances

Table 4-10   Distribution of modal utterances in the caregivers' data across time periods

Period	Age	Total no. utterances	Modal no.	Utterances % of total
Period 1	1; 4 to 1; 6	4 149	225	5.4%
Period 2	1; 7 to 1; 9	3 206	123	3.8%
Period 3	1; 10 to 2; 0	3 160	161	5.0%
Period 4	2; 1 to 2; 3	2 862	235	8.2%
Period 5	2; 4 to 2; 6	3 601	274	7.6%
Period 6	2; 7 to 2; 9	1 442	109	7.5%
Period 7	2; 10 to 3; 0	2 435	213	8.7%
Period 8	3; 1 to 3; 3	1 214	138	11.3%
Total	1; 4 to 3; 3	22 069	1 478	6.6%

in the caregivers' data and in the child's data across time periods showed similar trend of steady increase. The percentage of modal utterances in the caregivers' data increased from about 5% during period 1 to 11% during period 8, and the percentage of modal utterances in the child's data also increased from 0 during period 1 to 7% during period 8. Generally speaking, the frequencies of modal utterances in the caregivers' data were always higher than those in the child's data across time periods, with the exception of period 6 when the frequencies were the same (7.5%) in both data sets.

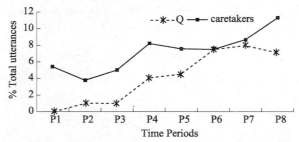

Figure 4-3   Distribution of modal utterances in the caregivers' data and in the
child's data across time periods

Modal utterances accounted for over 5% of total utterances in the caregivers' data during period 1, while the child did not start to produce modal utterances until the end of 1; 8 during period 2. This indicates that caregiver input may not be responsible for the late emergence of modals in the child's data. The trend of steady increase of modal utterances both in the caregivers' data and in the child's data indicates that caregivers adjust their input dynamically with the growth of the child.

2. Distribution of Modal Forms in the Caregivers' Data and in the Child's Data Across Time Periods

Table 4-11 shows the distribution of modal forms in the caregivers' data and in the child's data across time periods. From the above table, we can see the following pattern.

Table 4-11   Distribution of modal forms in the caregivers' data and in the child's data across time periods

		想 xiǎng %	会 huì %	要 yào %	敢 gǎn %	用 yòng %	愿意 yuàn yì %	能 néng %	可以 kěyǐ %	该 gāi %	得 děi %	喜欢 xǐ huan %	Total %
P1	C	20.0	20.4	22.4	9.8	1.5	1.1	16.9	1.1	0.7	5.5	0	100
	Q	0	0	0	0	0	0	0	0	0	0	0	0
P2	C	13.7	12.9	17.5	0.7	3.8	0.7	27.4	8.3	5.3	9.1	0	100
	Q	50	50	0	0	0	0	0	0	0	0	0	100
P3	C	7.1	14.2	23.6	1.1	0.5	2.9	26.6	11.2	5.9	6.5	0	100
	Q	19.0	14.2	28.5	0	4.7	4.7	9.5	9.5	9.5	0	0	100
P4	C	14.0	20.7	20.7	6.6	0.7	0.4	10.1	4.6	11.3	9.7	0.7	100
	Q	7.8	13.1	42.1	10.5	0	0	15.7	0	10.5	0	0	100
P5	C	12.7	18.7	16.9	0.7	2.4	1.4	17.6	6.0	6.3	16.9	0	100
	Q	48.1	9.2	13.8	0.9	0.9	0.9	14.8	0.9	3.7	5.5	0.9	100
P6	C	11.5	16.5	18.1	0.8	1.6	1.6	19.0	4.1	8.2	18.1	0	100
	Q	14.4	6.3	45	0.9	0	0	18.9	0	0.9	13.5	0	100
P7	C	13.6	17.6	17.6	0.4	4.4	0	22.0	8.8	2.2	9.6	3.5	100
	Q	20	10	29	1	0	0	25	3	0	4	8	100
P8	C	9.8	16.1	12.6	2.1	2.1	0	16.1	20.4	7.7	12.6	0	100
	Q	23.8	8.9	37.3	7.4	0	0	13.4	2.9	0	5.9	0	100
Total	C	13.3	17.8	19.0	3.2	2.1	1.0	18.6	7.3	5.8	10.8	0.6	100
	Q	25.4	10.1	30.9	2.6	0.4	0.4	17.3	1.7	2.4	6.3	1.9	100

Notes: C represents caregiver's data, and Q represents the child's data.

Firstly, modal forms that caregivers used frequently tended to be acquired early by the child. Modals 想 *xiǎng* 'desire' and 会 *huì* 'know how to, may' each accounted for a high percentage of 20% in the caregivers' data during period 1, which continued to occur frequently during period 2. 想 *xiǎng* 'desire' and 会 *huì* 'know how to' were the first modals acquired by the child.

Secondly, modal forms caregivers used infrequently tended to be acquired late by the child. Modals 可以 *kěyǐ* 'able to, may', 该 *gāi* 'should', 得 *děi* 'have to, must' and 喜欢 *xǐ huan* 'like' altogether accounted for a low percentage of less than 8% in the caregivers' data during period 1, which continued to occur infrequently during period 2. These modal forms were acquired late by the child.

Thirdly, high frequency did not always predict the child's early modal acquisition, while low frequency did not always predict the child's late modal acquisition. Modal 能 *néng* 'can' was one of the most frequently occurring modals in the caregivers' data, which accounted for a high frequency of near 17% during period 1 and about 27% during period 2 and 3. Modals 敢 *gǎn* 'dare', 用 *yòng* 'need to' and 愿意 *yuànyi* 'willing', on the other hand, altogether accounted for over 12% during period 1 and about 5% during period 2 and 3. Modal 能 *néng* 'can', however, was acquired later than 敢 *gǎn* 'dare', 用 *yòng* 'need to' and 愿意 *yuànyi* 'willing' by the child.

Fourthly, total frequencies of modals in the caregivers' data generally agreed with those in the child's data. The 11 modal forms can be divided into three groups in terms of relative frequency. The first group consists modals 想 *xiǎng* 'desire', 会 *huì* 'know how to, may' and 要 *yào* 'want, must' and 能 *néng* 'can' which occupied high frequencies both in the caregivers' data (58.7%) and in the child's data (83.7%). The second group consisted of 得 *děi* 'have to, must', 可以 *kěyǐ* 'able to, may' and 该 *gāi* 'should', which were less frequent both in the caregivers' data (23.9%) and in the child's data (10.4%). The third group consists of 敢 *gǎn* 'dare', 用 *yòng* 'need to', 愿意 *yuànyì* 'willing' and 喜欢 *xǐhuān* 'like' which were the least frequent both in the caregivers' data (6.9%) and in the child's data (5.3%).

Studies on the relation between caregiver input and modal acquisition show that there exist partial relation between mothers' input frequency and the order of acquisition of modal forms by children. Wells's study (1979) and Shatz and Wilcox's study (1991) reveal that modals *can* and *will*, the two forms acquired first in many children, were the modals that English-speaking mothers used frequently when talking with their children. Choi (1991) found partial relation between input frequency and the acquisition order of Korean SE suffixes in three mother-child pairs. Korean mothers used the suffix *-e* most frequently followed by *-ci*, *-ta*, and *-tay*, in that order. In the children's speech, however, *-ta* was first acquired followed by *-e*. The forms *-ci* and *-tay* were acquired third and last respectively. The semantic and pragmatic salience of -ta may be the reason for its earlier acquisition. Choi proposes that both input frequency and the child's own cognitive abilities at the time of acquisition contribute to the early acquisition of modal suffixes in Korean. Aksu-Koç (1998) also reports partial relation between input frequency and the acquisition order of Turkish sentence-ending verbal suffixes in one mother-child pair. The child acquired *-dI* before *-Iyor*, whereas *-Iyor* was much more frequent than *-dI* in the mother's speech. The authors explains that the early acquisition of -dI may be due to its semantic and pragmatic salience. The present study also reveals partial relation between input frequency and acquisition order. Modal 敢 *gǎn* 'dare', 用 *yòng* 'need to' and 愿意 *yuànyì* 'willing' were acquired early in spite of their low frequencies in caregivers' input, while 能 *néng* 'can' was acquired late in spite of its high frequencies in caregivers' input. This disparity may be due to the semantic features of modals, which will be discussed in detail in the next section.

The above discussion revealing the percentages of modal utterances in the caregivers' data showed a steady trend of increase with the growth of the child, which were always higher than those in the child's data. There exist certain partial relation between the caregivers' input frequencies of modals and the order of acquisition of modals by children.

4.4.2 Distribution of Semantics of Modals in the Caregivers' Data and in the Child's Data Across Time Periods

In this section, the distributional patterns of semantics of modals in the caregivers' data across time periods are investigated, which are further compared with those features in the child's data. First, the distributional patterns of modal categories in the caregivers' data are investigated, and then compared with those in the child's data. Second, the distributional patterns of semantic categories of modal forms in the caregivers' data across time periods are investigated, and then compared with those in the child's data. Third, the semantic features of modals in the caregivers' data are investigated, and then compared with those in the child's data.

1. Distribution of Modal Categories in the Caregivers' Data and in the Child's Data Across Time Periods

Figure 4-4 shows the evolution of dynamic, deontic and epistemic modals in the caregivers' data across time periods. Dynamic modals started to be the most frequent category of modality, taking up for over 60% of all modal uses during period 1, which dropped to 38% during period 2 and then revealed a trend of fluctuations around 45% during the remaining periods. Deontic modals were used less frequently than dynamic modals at the very beginning, accounting for 30% of all modal uses, which surged to 60% during period 2, decreased to 52% during period 3, and then revealed a trend of fluctuations around 40% during the remaining periods. Epistemic modals were used the least frequently from the beginning, taking up for only almost 6% of modal uses during period 1, which fell to under 1% during period 2, and then showed a trend of steady rise to almost 15% during period 8. Generally speaking, dynamic modals (49.1%) and deontic modals (40.9%) were more frequently occurring than epistemic modals (9.3%) in the caregivers' data during all time periods. This pattern agrees with the distribution of dynamic modals (70%), deontic modals (24%) and epistemic modals (4%) in the child's data.

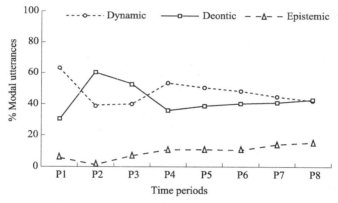

Figure 4-4   Distribution of modal categories in the caregivers' data across time periods

Figure 4-5, 4-6 and 4-7 compare the distributional patterns of dynamic, deontic and epistemic modals in the caregivers' data and in the child's data across time periods respectively. From these figures, we can see the following patterns. Firstly, generally speaking, the distribution of modal categories in both data sets showed similar patterns: dynamic modals were the most frequently occurring modal category, followed by deontic modals, and epistemic modals were the least frequently occurring modal category. Secondly, dynamic modals were less frequently occurring in the caregivers' data than in the child's data, whereas deontic modals and epistemic modals were more frequently occurring in the caregivers' data than in the child's data.

Thirdly, dynamic, deontic and epistemic modals in both data sets showed similar developmental patterns.

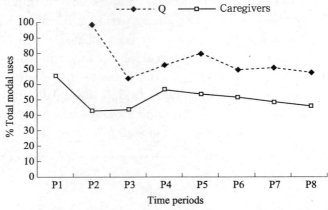

Figure 4-5   Distribution of dynamic modals in the caregivers' data and in the child's data across time periods

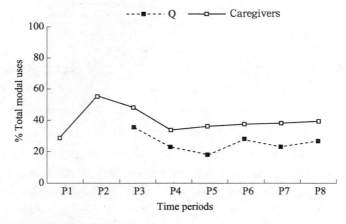

Figure 4-6   Distribution of deontic modals in the caregivers' data and in the child's data across time periods

Distribution of modal categories in the caregivers' speech may be related to the acquisition of modals. Shatz and Wilcox (1991) discover that epistemic modals were acquired late and used infrequently by children may be due to the infrequent use of epistemic modals in caregivers' speech (10%). The present study also finds that epistemic modals were used infrequently (9%) by caregivers and acquired late by the child.

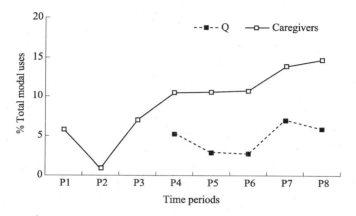

Figure 4-7   Distribution of epistemic modals in the caregivers' data and in the
child's data across time periods

2. Distribution of Semantic Categories of Modal Forms in the Caregivers' Data and in the Child's Data Across Time Periods

From Table 4-12, we can see the detailed semantic distributional patterns of modals in the caregivers' data and in the child's data across time periods. Firstly, the percentages of the semantic categories of each modal form across time periods were constantly changing both in the caregivers' data and in the child's data, which shows that the development of the semantics of modals is a dynamic process. For example, in both data sets, the dynamic use of 会 *huì* 'know how to' showed a general trend of decrease, and its epistemic use showed a general trend of increase. The deontic use of 得 *děi* 'have to' showed a general trend of decrease in the caregivers' data, whereas in the child's data it showed a trend of increase.

Table 4-12 Distribution of the semantic categories of each modal form in the caregivers' data and in the child's data across time periods

Modal forms	Modal categories	P1 %	P2 %	P3 %	P4 %	P5 %	P6 %	P7 %	P8 %	Total %
想 xiǎng	DY (C)	100	100	100	100	100	100	100	100	100
	DY (Q)	0	100	100	100	100	100	100	100	100
会 huì	DY (C)	80.8	100	66.7	62.3	60.4	55	40	30.4	61.7
	DY (Q)	0	100	100	80	70	57.1	30	66.7	65.2
	EP (C)	19.2	0	33.3	37.7	39.6	45	60	69.6	38.3
	EP (Q)	0	0	0	20	30	42.9	70	33.3	34.8
要 yào	DY (C)	49.1	26.1	57.5	56.6	66.7	86.4	65	66.7	58.5
	DY (Q)	0	0	66.7	93.8	86.7	90	79.3	56	80.9
	DE (C)	43.9	69.6	35	37.7	27.1	13.6	32.5	33.3	36.5
	DE (Q)	0	0	33.3	0	13.3	10	20.7	36	17
	EP (C)	7	4.3	7.5	5.7	6.2	0	2.5	0	5
	EP (Q)	0	0	0	6.2	0	0	0	8	2.1
敢 gǎn	DY (C)	100	100	100	100	100	100	100	100	100
	DY (Q)	0	0	0	100	100	100	100	100	100
用 yòng	DY (C)	0	0	0	0	0	0	0	0	0
	DY (Q)	0	0	0	0	0	0	0	0	0
	DE (C)	100	100	100	100	100	100	100	100	100
	DE (Q)	0	0	100	0	100	0	0	0	100
愿意 yuànyi	DY (C)	100	100	100	100	100	100	0	0	100
	DY (Q)	0	0	100	0	100	0	0	0	100
能 néng	DY (C)	25.6	11.1	8.9	15.4	22	43.5	28	65.2	24.7
	DY (Q)	0	0	0	16.7	25	38.1	56	44.4	39.2
	DE (C)	74.4	88.9	88.9	69.2	88	39.1	60	21.7	69.3
	DE (Q)	0	0	100	83.3	75	61.9	44	55.6	60.8
	EP (C)	0	0	2.2	15.4	0	17.4	12	13.1	6
	EP (Q)	0	0	0	0	0	0	0	0	0
可以 kěyǐ	DY (C)	33.3	9.1	21.1	58.3	70.6	20	10	17.2	28.4
	DY (Q)	0	0	50	0	100	0	0	50	37.5
	DE (C)	66.7	90.9	78.9	41.7	29.4	80	90	82.8	71.6
	DE (Q)	0	0	50	0	0	0	100	50	62.5
该 gāi	DE (C)	100	100	100	100	77.8	100	100	81.8	93.5
	DE (Q)	0	0	100	100	100	100	0	0	100
	EP (C)	0	0	0	0	22.2	0	0	18.2	6.5
	EP (Q)	0	0	0	0	0	0	0	0	0

										Continued
Modal forms	Modal categories	P1 %	P2 %	P3 %	P4 %	P5 %	P6 %	P7 %	P8 %	Total %
得 děi	DY (C)	0	25	18.2	28	29.2	4.5	18.2	22.2	20.3
	DY (Q)	0	0	0	0	83.3	6.7	0	0	20.7
	DE (C)	92.9	75	81.8	82	66.7	95.5	77.3	77.8	77.4
	DE (Q)	0	0	0	0	16.7	93.3	100	100	79.3
	EP (C)	7.1	0	0	0	4.1	0	4.5	0	2.3
	EP (Q)	0	0	0	0	0	0	0	0	0
喜欢 xǐhuan	DY (C)	0	0	0	100	0	0	100	0	100
	DY (Q)	0	0	0	0	100	0	100	0	100

Secondly, the general distributional patterns of the semantic categories of modals in the caregivers' data were consistent with those in the child's data. Some modals were predominantly dynamic in both data sets, such as 会 *huì* 'know how to, may' and 要 *yào* 'want, must'. Some modals were predominantly deontic in both data sets, such as 能 *néng* 'can', 可以 *kěyǐ* 'able to, may', 该 *gāi* 'should' and 得 *děi* 'have to, must'. Modal 用 *yòng* 'need to' was only used as a deontic modal in both data sets.

Thirdly, some uses of modals by caregivers were not acquired by the child until the end of the investigation. Caregivers started to produce epistemic modal 得 *děi* 'must' utterances since period 1, for example, 它再尿床, 你又是打屁屁, 它不得哭吗 *tā zài niào chuáng, nǐ yòu shì dǎ pìpi, tā bù děi kū ma* 'you will spank it if it pees on bed again. Must it not cry?' (*GRM V 2; 4.04). Caregivers started to produce epistemic modal 能 *néng* utterances since period 3, for example, 下雨怎么能晒干呢 *xiàyǔ zěnme néng shàigān ne* 'how can it be dried when it is raining' (*FAT V 2; 8.17) since period 3. The child did not acquire these uses until she was 3; 3.

Dynamic, deontic and epistemic modality can be realized in different modal forms. Are these modal forms equally frequent in expressing certain modal category in the caregivers' data? If not, which modal forms are more frequently used? Which modal forms are less frequently used? The percentages of each modal form in expressing dynamic, deontic and epistemic modalities in the caregivers' data and in the child's data are presented in Table 4-13.

When used as dynamic modals, 想 *xiǎng* 'desire', 会 *huì* 'know how to', 要 *yào* 'want' and 能 *néng* 'can' were the most frequently occurring modal forms in the caregivers' data, accounting for over 80% of all dynamic modal uses. These four modal forms were also the most frequently occurring dynamic modals in the child's data, accounting for over 90% of all modal uses. Dynamic modals 敢 *gǎn* 'dare', 愿意 *yuànyì* 'willing', 可以 *kěyǐ* 'able to', 得 *děi* 'have to' and 喜欢 *xǐhuan* 'like' were infrequent in both data sets.

When used as deontic modals, 要 *yào* 'must', 能 *néng* 'can' and 得 *děi* 'have to' were the most frequently occurring modal forms, taking up over 68% of all deontic modal uses in the caregivers' data. These four modals were also the most frequently occurring modals in the child's data, accounting for 84% of all deontic modal uses. Deontic modal 能 *néng* 'can' was the most frequently occurring modals in both data sets. Deontic modals 用 *yòng* 'need to', 可以 *kěyǐ* 'may' and 该 *gāi* 'should' were infrequent in both data sets.

Table 4-13   Distribution of the semantic categories of each modal form in the caregivers' data and in the child's data

		DY %	DE %	EP %
想 *xiǎng*	C	27.2	×	×
	Q	35.9	×	×
会 *huì*	C	22.3	×	71.5
	Q	9.3	×	84.2
要 *yào*	C	22.5	16.9	9.9
	Q	35.3	21.2	15.8
敢 *gǎn*	C	6.7	×	×
	Q	3.7	×	×
用 *yòng*	C	0	5.2	×
	Q	0	1.8	×

		DY %	DE %	EP %
愿意 yuànyì	C	2	×	×
	Q	0.6	×	×
能 néng	C	9.3	31.5	11.9
	Q	9.6	42.5	0
可以 kěyǐ	C	4.2	12.8	×
	Q	0.9	4.4	×
该 gāi	C	×	13.2	4
	Q	×	9.7	0
得 děi	C	4.5	20.4	2.7
	Q	1.9	20.4	0
喜欢 xǐhuan	C	1.3	×	×
	Q	2.8	×	×
Total	C	100	100	100
	Q	100	100	100

Continued

Epistemic modal 会 huì 'may' was the most frequently occurring modal form both in the caregivers' data (71.5%) and in the child's data (84.2%). The epistemic use of 能 néng 'can' and 得 děi 'must' were not acquired by the child.

The distributional patterns of the three categories of modal forms are generally consistent with those in the child's data. Frequent modal forms of certain semantic category in the caregivers' data tended to occur frequently in the child's data, while infrequent modal forms of certain semantic category in the caregivers' data tended to occur infrequently in the child's data.

3. Semantic Features of Modals in the Caregivers' Data and in the Child's Data

The semantic features of the three categories of modals in the caregivers' data are investigated, which are then compared with those features in the child's data.

1) Semantic Features of Dynamic Modals in the Caregivers' Data and in the Child's Data

Dynamic modals are divided into three groups to investigate their semantic features. The first group consists of 想 *xiǎng* 'desire', 要 *yào* 'want', 喜欢 *xǐhuan* 'like', 愿意 *yuànyì* 'willing' and 敢 *gǎn* 'dare' which express the notion of desire. The second group consists of 会 *huì* 'know how to', 能 *néng* 'can' and 可以 *kěyǐ* 'able to' which express the notion of ability. The third group consists of 用 *yòng* 'need to' and 得 *děi* 'have to' which express the notion of need.

想 *xiǎng* 'desire', 要 *yào* 'want', 喜欢 *xǐhuan* 'like', 愿意 *yuànyì* 'willing' & 敢 *gǎn* 'dare'

Modals 想 *xiǎng* 'desire' and 要 *yào* 'want' each took up over 20% of all dynamic modal uses in the caregivers' data, while 喜欢 *xǐhuan* 'like', 愿意 *yuànyì* 'willing' and 敢 *gǎn* 'dare' altogether took up 10% of all dynamic modal uses.

Most (67.3%) dynamic modal 想 *xiǎng* 'desire' utterances in the caregivers' data were used to inquire about the child's desires (37).

(37) (There is a puppy on the road. Mommy puts the child on the ground to let her play with the puppy, while the child cries and wants to be picked up.) A 1; 4.04
MOT: 想　　让　　妈妈　　抱着　　去　看?
　　　xiǎng　*ràng*　*māma*　*bàozhe*　*qù*　*kàn?*
　　　Desire　let　mommy　hold　go　look at
　　　'(Do you) want to look at the (puppy) while mommy holds you in the arm?'

Many (45.7%) dynamic modal 要 *yào* 'want' utterances in the caregivers' data were used to describe the child's actions (38) or inquire about the child's desires (39):

(38) (The child put the belt of mommy's bag around her neck.) V

1; 6.16

FAT: 哦, 你　要　　　背　　呀。

Ò, nǐ　yào　　bēi　　ya.

oh, you　want　carry　P

'Oh, you want to carry (the bag).'

(39) (The child wants to climb down the sliding board.) A 1; 4.04

MOT: 你　要　　下去　　吗?

Nǐ　yào　　xiàqù　　ma?

you　want　go down　P

'Do you want to climb down (the sliding board)?'

Most (70%) dynamic 喜欢 xǐhuan 'like' utterances were used to describe the child's enjoyment in doing something (40), or inquire about the child's likes or dislikes (41).

(40) (Mommy is talking with the child's aunt.) V 2; 1.16

MOT: 这个 芊芊　　就喜欢 看 虫子, 看　　吃　的。

Zhège Qiān Qian jiù xǐhuan kàn chóngzi, kàn　chī　de.

this Qian Qian EMP like look worm　look　eat　P

'This Qian Qian just likes to look at worms and stuff to eat.'

(41) (Mommy is talking with the child.) V 2; 10.01

MOT: 那　你　喜欢　吃　什么　呀?

Nà　nǐ　xǐhuan　chī　shénme　ya?

then　you　like　eat　what　P

'Then what do you like to eat?'

Half (50%) of the 愿意 yuànyi 'willing' utterances in the caregivers' data were used to inquire about the child's willingness (42).

(42) (The child refuses to walk.) V 2; 1.22

MOT: 你 要 不　愿意　走　就　回家　玩　吧?

Nǐ　yào　bú　yuànyi　zǒu　jiù　huíjiā　wán　ba?

you if not willing walk then   go back home play P
'If you are not willing to walk, would you go back
home to play?'

Most (69%) 敢 *gǎn* 'dare' utterances in the caregivers' data were
used to inquire about the child's courage (43):

(43) (The child asks to go out to play.) V 2; 2.19
GRM: 下着   大   雨，   你   敢   出去   不   敢？
Xiàzhe dà   yǔ,   nǐ   gǎn chūqu bù   gǎn?
fall   big rain,   you dare go out   not   dare
'It's raining heavily outside. Do you dare to go out?'

会 *huì* 'know how to', 能 *néng* 'can' & 可以 *kěyǐ* 'able to'

会 *huì* 'know how to' was one of the most frequently occurring
dynamic modal forms, accounting for 22% of all dynamic modal uses
in the caregivers' data. 能 néng 'can' and 可以 *kěyǐ* 'able to' accounted
for 9% and 4% respectively.

Most (75%) 会 *huì* 'know how to' utterances in the caregivers'
data were used to describe the child's acquired skills (44).

(44) (The child learned to climb down the bed.) V 1; 5.17
FAT: 芊芊   会   下   床   了。
Qiān Qian huì   xià   chuáng le.
Qian Qian can   climb down bed   PHA
'Qian Qian can climb down the bed now.'

Most (61%) 能 *néng* 'can' utterances in the caregivers' data were
used to describe or inquire the child's ability, as in (45) and (46)
respectively.

(45) (The child fails to reach the building block while sitting on
the bed. Mommy moves her closer to the building block.) V
3; 1.06

MOT: 这样　坐　才　能　　拿　　东西。

Zhèyang zuò cái néng ná dōngxi.

this   way sit CONJ can   take stuff

'You can reach the stuff only by sitting this way.'

(46) (The child wants to enter a door on the sliding board.) A 1; 4.04

MOT: 你　能　不　能　　进去　呀?

Nǐ néng bù néng jìnqù ya?

you can not can   enter P

'Can you enter the door?'

Many (44%) 可以 kěyǐ 'able to' utterances were used to express the natural property of something or the ability of somebody, as in (47).

(47) (Mommy and the child are making candies and bowls with Plasticine.) A 2; 2.27

*MOT: 咱们　　有　　一　个　大的　碗,

Zánmen yǒu yí gè dàde wǎn.

we   have one PL big   bowl

就　可以　装　　很多　　很多　糖豆儿。

jiù kěyǐ zhuāng hěn duō hěn duō tángdòuer.

CONJ can hold   very many very many candy

'If we have a big bowl, (it) can hold many candies. '

用 yòng 'need to' & 得 děi 'have to'

Modal 用 yòng 'need to' can be used as a dynamic modal as well as a deontic modal, while in the caregivers' data 用 yòng 'need to' was not used as a dynamic modal. 得 děi 'have to' accounted for over 4% of all dynamic modal uses in the caregivers' data.

Most (74%) dynamic modal 得 děi 'have to' utterances in the caregivers' data were used to describe need of the child (48).

(48) (The child lies in bed to take a rest after she has been playing for a while.) V 2; 6.16

*MOT: 哦，　你　　还　　得　　躺　这儿　歇歇　呀　你?

　　　Ò,　 nǐ　 hái　 děi　tǎng zhè er xiēxie ya nǐ?

　　　oh,　you　EMP　must lie　here　rest P　 you

　　　'Oh, you must lie down here to take a rest?'

Generally speaking, most (62%) dynamic modal utterances in the caregivers' data were used to describe or inquire about the child's desires, abilities, needs, etc., whereas most (65%) dynamic modal utterances in the child's data were used to describe her own desires, abilities, needs, etc.

2) Semantic Features of Deontic Modals in the Caregivers' Data and in the Child's Data

Deontic modals are divided into three groups to investigate their semantic features. The first group consists of 要 *yào* 'must', 该 *gāi* 'should' and 得 *děi* 'have to' which express the notion of obligation. The second group consists of 能 *néng* 'can' and 可以 *kěyǐ* 'may' which express the notion of permission. The third group consists of 用 *yòng* 'need to' which expresses the notion of need.

要 *yào* 'must', 该 *gāi* 'should' & 得 *děi* 'have to'

Deontic modals 要 *yào* 'must', 该 *gāi* 'should' and 得 *děi* 'have to' all occurred quite frequently in the caregivers' data.

As has been mentioned earlier, 要 *yào* was mainly used as a dynamic modal (58.5%) in the caregivers' data, followed by deontic modal uses (36.5%). As a deontic modal, 要 *yào* 'must' utterances in the caregivers' data were mainly (68%) used in the negative form 不要 *bú yào* 'not must', expressing adult's prohibition on the child's action (49).

(49) (The child takes mommy's glasses.) A 2; 5.31

　　MOT: 不　要　拿　　眼镜。

> *Bú yào ná yǎnjìng.*
> not must take glasses
> 'Do not take my glasses.'

Many (35%) deontic modal 该 *gāi* 'should' utterances were used to express routines (50).

(50) (After dinner, daddy plays with the child) V 2; 8.17

> *FAT: 快 一 点 了, 该 睡觉 啦。
> *Kuài yì diǎn le, gāi shuìjiào le.*
> almost one o'clock P, should sleep P
> '(It's) almost one o'clock and it's time to take a nap.'

Most (56%) deontic modal 得 *děi* 'have to' utterances were used to express the child's obligations (51).

(51) (The child wants to wear new shoes.) V 1; 5.28

> *MOT: 芊芊 你 得 先 洗 脚。
> *Qiān Qian nǐ děi xiān xǐ jiǎo.*
> Qian Qian you have to first wash feet
> 'Qian Qian, you have to wash your feet first.'

能 *néng* 'can' & 可以 *kěyǐ* 'may'

Deontic modal 能 *néng* 'can' was the most frequently occurring deontic modal form (31.5%). In contrast to the high frequency of 能 *néng* 'can', 可以 *kěyǐ* 'may' which also expresses permission, was only used for 12.8% among all the deontic modal utterances in caregivers' data.

能 *néng* 'can' was mainly (84%) used in its negative form 不能 *bù néng* 'can not', expressing adult's prohibition on the child's action (52).

(52) (Grandma plays hide and seek with the child. The child can not find her and wants to cry.) A 2; 5.31

> *MOT: 哎, 不 能 哭, 不 能 哭。咱俩 去 找找。
> *Ai, bù néng kū, bù néng kū. Zánliǎ qù zhǎozhǎo.*

Hey, not can   cry, not can   cry. We   go   seek

'Hey, do not cry. Do not cry. Let's look for her.'

Many (35%) 可以 *kěyǐ* 'may' utterances were used to expressing the adult's permission on the child's action (53):

(53) (The child and mommy play plasticene together.) V 2; 11.18

    *MOT: 你　可以　再　　找　　　绿　颜色。

       Nǐ　*kěyǐ*　*zài*　　*zhǎo*　　*lǜ*　*yánsè.*

       you may　again　look for　green　color

       'You may look for green plasticene again.'

用 *yòng* 'need to'

Deontic modal 用 *yòng* 'need to' only accounted for 5.2% of all deontic modal uses. As has been discussed earlier, 用 *yòng* 'need to' was only used as a deontic modal in the caregivers' data. Most (68%) deontic 用 *yòng* 'need to' utterances were in the negative form 不 用 *bú yòng* 'not need to', canceling the child's actions (54).

(54) (The child insists on washing her socks which are obviously clean.) V 1; 7.09

    *MOT: 不　用　　洗。

       Bú　*yòng*　*xǐ.*

       not　need　wash

       'You need not wash (the socks).'

Generally speaking, most (65%) deontic modal utterances in the caregivers' data were used to give permission or prohibition to the child's actions, and most (58%) of these utterances in the child's data were also used to give permission or prohibition to others' actions.

3) Semantic Features of Epistemic Modals in the Caregivers' Data

Epistemic modals are divided into two groups to investigate their semantic features. The first group consists of 会 *huì* 'may' and 能 *néng* 'can' which express the notion of epistemic possibility. The second group consists of 要 *yào* 'must', 该 *gāi* 'should' and 得 *děi* 'must' which express the notion of epistemic necessity.

会 *huì* 'may' & 能 *néng* 'can'

Epistemic modal 会 *huì* 'may' accounted for over 71% of all epistemic modal uses in the caregivers' data, and 能 *néng* 'can' only accounted for less than 12%. Many (47%) epistemic 会 *huì* 'may' utterances and most (78%) 能 *néng* 'can' utterances in the caregivers' data were used to inquire the likelihood of certain occurrences, as in (55) and (56).

(55) (The child is chasing after a balloon and tries to stamp on it.)
V 1; 5.15
*MOT: 踩   了   会   怎么样?
         Cǎi   le   huì   zěnmeyàng?
         stamp PHA may   how
         'What may happen if (you) stamp on it?'

(56) (The child puts her feet in grandpa's shoes.) A 2; 2.27
*GRM: 那么 小的   脚   能   穿   这么   大的 鞋   吗?
        Nàme xiǎode jiǎo néng chuān zhème dàde xié   ma?
        that little   foot can fit   this big shoe   P
        'Can the little feet fit those big shoes?'

要 *yào* 'must', 该 *gāi* 'should' & 得 *děi* 'must'

Epistemic modal 要 *yào* 'must' accounted for less than 10% of all epistemic modal uses in the caregivers' data, 该 *gāi* 'should' for 4%, and 得 *děi* 'must' for less than 3%. Epistemic modal 要 *yào* 'must', 该 *gāi* 'should' and 得 *děi* 'must' utterances were used to express the speaker's estimation on the probability of certain occurrences, as in (57), (58) and (59).

(57) (The child tears at mommy's sweater.) V 1; 10.27

　　*MOT: 不行, 妈妈的 衣服 都要 被 你 给 撕坏 了。

　　　　Bù xíng, māmade yīfu　dōu yào bèi　nǐ　gěi　sī huài le.

　　　　not OK, mommy's clothes EMP must by you by tear worn PHA

　　　　'No, mommy's sweater must be torn to shreds by you.'

(58) (The child is drawing a picture for her teacher.) V 3; 2.11

　　*GRM: 老师 心里 该 多 高兴 啊!

　　　　Lǎoshī　xīnlǐ　gāi　duō　gāoxìng　a!

　　　　teacher　heart　should　very　happy　P

　　　　'How happy the teacher should be (on seeing the drawing)!'

(59) (The child is playing house with a doll. She says the doll has peed on the sheet and intends to spank her.) V 2; 4.04

　　*GRM: 她 再 尿 床, 你 又是 打屁屁,

　　　　Tā　zài　niào　chuáng, nǐ　yòushì　dǎpìpi,

　　　　She again　pee　sheet,　you　again　spank,

　　　　她 不 得 哭 吗?

　　　　tā　bù　děi　kū　ma?

　　　　she　not　must　cry　P?

　　　　'You will spank her if she pees on the sheet again. She must cry then?'

Generally speaking, epistemic modal utterances in the caregivers' data were used to inquire or describe the likelihood or probability of certain occurrences. In the child's data, epistemic modal 会 *huì* 'may' and 要 *yào* 'must' utterances expressed similar meanings, while epistemic modal 能 *néng* 'can' and 得 *děi* 'must' utterances were non-existent.

To sum up, the distributional patterns of modal categories in the caregivers' data generally agree with those in the child's data.

Dynamic modals were the most frequently occurring category in the caregivers' data, followed by deontic modals, and epistemic modals were the least frequently occurring category. This distributional pattern agrees with that in the child's data. Furthermore, the distributional patterns of semantic categories of modal forms in both data sets showed similar patterns. The semantic features of modal utterances in the caregivers' data showed similarities as well as differences from those in the child's data.

4.4.3 Distribution of the Syntactic Structures of Modal Utterances in the Caregivers' Data and in the Child's Data Across Time Periods

In this section, the syntactic structures in the caregivers' data, the relation between modal categories and sentence types, and the relation between modal categories and subjecthood are investigated in detail, which will be further compared with those features in the child's data.

1. Syntactic Structures of Modal Utterances in the Caregivers' Data and in the Child's Data

First, sentence types were diverse in the caregivers' data since period 1. Declaratives as well as interrogatives were present since the beginning of the investigation. Interrogatives accounted for about 30% in all modal utterances in the caregivers' data in various constructions, such as [Modal+VP] with a rising intonation (60), or [Modal+不 *bù* 'not' + Mod+VP?] (61), or [Modal+VP+啊/吧/吗/呀 *ā/bā/mā/yā*?] (62), or [为什么 *wèishénme* 'why'+Modal+VP?] (63), and so on.

(60) (There is a puppy on the road. Mommy puts the child on the ground to let her play with the puppy, but the child starts to cry and wants to be picked up.) A 1; 4.04

*MOT: 想　　　让　妈妈　抱着　　　去　看?

Xiǎng ràng māma   bàozhe   qù   kàn?

desire let   mommy   hold in arms go   look

'(Do you) want mommy hold you in my arms to look (at the puppy).'

(61) (The child puts her hands on the fridge.) V 1; 4.10

    *MOT: 想   不   想   吃饭?

        Xiǎng bù xiǎng   chīfàn?

        desire not desire   eat

        'Do you want to eat?'

(62) (The child wants to climb down the sliding board.) A 1; 4.04

    *MOT: 你   要   下去   吗?

        nǐ   yào   xiàqu   ma?

        You   want   go down · P

        'Do you want to climb down?'

(63) (Mommy touches the child's face with a ball. The child points to her face and said the ball has bitten her.) V 1; 6.23

    *MOT: 它   怎么   会   咬   你   呢?

        Tā zěnme huì yǎo nǐ   ne?

        it   how   can bite you P

        'How can it bite you?'

Second, subjects of modal utterances were diverse in the caregivers' data since period 1, such as personal pronouns, phrases and clauses. Of all the modal utterances with personal pronouns as their subjects, the second personal pronoun 你 *nǐ* 'you' was the most frequently occurring subject (64%), most of which referred to the child. Examples of modal utterances with different subjects are given as follows.

(64) (The child is playing in the kindergarten) A 1; 4.04

    *MOT: 芊芊,   你   要   不   要   坐   滑梯   啊?

        Qiān Qian nǐ   yào   bú   yào   zuò   huátī   a?

Qian Qian you want not want sit slide P
'Do you want to slide down or not, Qian Qian?'

(65) (The child wants to climb down the sliding board) A 1; 4.04
*MOT: 这个　　地方　　不　　能　　下。
Zhège dìfāng bù néng xià.
this place not can down
'(You) can not climb down (the sliding board) from this place.'

Third, verbs of modal utterances in caregivers' data were diverse since period 1. Various modal forms were existent from the beginning of the investigation, such as positive modal forms, negative modal forms, as well as the [Mod+不 bù 'not' +Mod] constructions (66). Different adverbs were frequently occurring before modals (67). Complex structures, such as 把 bǎ clause (68) and 给 gěi clause (69), were also quite frequent after modals.

(66) (The child is playing with mommy at home.) V 1; 4.10
*MOT: 想　　不　　想　　去　　操场　　　　玩儿？
Xiǎng bù xiǎng qù cāochǎng wán er?
desire not desire go playground play
'Do you want to go to the playground to play?'

(67) (The child picks a bag of candy from the shelf in the supermarket.) A 1; 4.04
*MOT: 你　　还　　想　　要　　什么？
Nǐ hái xiǎng yào shénme?
you Adv desire want what
'What else do you want?'

(68) (The child walks toward the doll.) V 1; 4.25
*MOT: 芊芊　　你想　　不想　　把　娃娃　拿　起来？
Qiān Qian nǐ xiǎng bù xiǎng bǎ wáwa ná qǐlái?
Qian Qian you desire not desire Executive Marker doll

take up?

'Qian Qian, do you want to take up the doll?'

(69) (The child holds a camera in her hand.) V 1; 5.15

    *MOT: 你　会不会　　给　　妈妈　　照相　　　啊　宝贝？

        Nǐ　huì bú huì　gěi　māma　zhàoxiàng　a　bǎobèi?

        You can not can Executive Marker mommy take a

        picture P baby

        'Can you take a picture for mommy, baby?'

Fourthly, objects of modal utterances in the caregivers' data were also diverse from period 1, such as phrases (70) and clauses (71).

(70) (The child is playing with mommy) V 1; 5.15

    *MOT: 你会　不　会唱　　那个　　两　　只老虎？

        Nǐ huì　bú　huì chàng　nàge　liǎng　zhī lǎohǔ?

        you can　not　can sing　that　two　PL tiger

        'Can you sing the two tigers?'

(71) (The child puts her feet on the floor) V 1; 7.09

    *GRM: 现在　不　能　　放　地　上　了，脚　凉。

        Xiànzài bù néng　fàng dì　shàng le,　jiǎo liáng.

        now　not can　put floor on　P,　foot　cold

        'Now (you) can not put (your feet) on the floor,

        (because) your feet will turn cold.'

The structures of modal utterances in the caregivers' data were diverse from the beginning of the investigation. Those structures in the child's data, in contrast, developed from simple constructions to complex constructions gradually. Sentence types in the caregivers' data including declaratives as well as interrogatives in various forms since period 1, while sentence types in the child's data developed from declaratives to interrogatives gradually. Subjects, verbs and objects of modal utterances in the caregivers' data include complex constructions since period 1, whereas those structures in the child's data diversified gradually.

2. Sentence Types and Modal Categories in the Caregivers' Data and in the Child's Data

In this section, the relationship between sentence types and modal categories in the caregivers' data is investigated and then compared with that in the child's data.

From Table 4-14, we can see the following patterns. Firstly, most modals in the caregivers' data were in affirmatives or interrogatives. Compared with modal uses in the child's data, more modals in the caregivers' data appeared in interrogatives and less in affirmatives. Secondly, both in the caregivers' data and in the child's data, deontic modals were more likely to occur in negatives than dynamic and epistemic modals were.

Table 4-14　Sentence types and modal categories in the caregivers' data and in the child's data

Sentence types		DY %	DE %	EP %
Affirmatives	C	49.2	45.5	39
	Q	76.3	53	89.4
Negatives	C	12.4	44.2	13.6
	Q	15.6	41.7	10.5
Interrogatives	C	38.3	10.2	47.2
	Q	8.1	5.3	0

Why did affirmatives account for lower percentages in the caregivers' data than those in the child's data, whereas interrogatives accounted for higher percentages in the caregivers' data than those in the child's data? It seems that the question-answer interaction pattern between caregivers and the child is partly related to the above pattern. Caregivers were more likely to raise questions in interrogatives, and therefore the child was more likely to answer questions in affirmatives or negatives. For example, when mommy asked 你会捏啥 *nǐ huì niē shá* 'what can you make' while playing Plasticene with the child, the child answered 不会捏捏 *bú huì nīenie* '(I) can not make (anything)'. Another reason for the higher frequencies of interrogatives in the caregivers' data might be that interrogatives are syntactically complex and therefore pose greater challenge for the child to acquire. It is worth noting that the child did not produce one interrogative utterance containing epistemic modals, while near 50% epistemic modal utterances in the caregivers' data were interrogatives, for example mommy asked the child (蚊子) 进来了会怎么样啊 *(wénzi) jìnlái le huì zěnmeyàng a* 'what will happen if mosquitoes get inside' while they were tucking in the mosquito net.

3. Subjecthood and Modal Categories in the Caregivers' Data and in the Child's Data

In this section, the relationship between subjecthood and modal categories in the caregivers' data is investigated and then compared with that in the child's data.

From Table 4-15, we can see the following patterns. Firstly, a large percentage of dynamic modal utterances in the caregivers' data had subjects referring to others (76%), most (61%) of which referred to the child in the form of 芊芊 *Qiān Qian* or 你 *nǐ* 'you'. These dynamic modal utterances were used to describe or inquire the child's abilities, intentions or desires. For example, 你还想要什么 *nǐ hái xiǎng yào shénme* 'what else do you want to have' (*MOT A 1; 4.04). The subjects of dynamic modal utterances in the child's data, in contrast, were mainly (65%) referring to the child herself in the forms of her own name 芊芊 *Qiān Qian* or 我 *wǒ* 'I', and these utterances were used to describe the child's own abilities, intentions or desires. The difference might be related to the fact that the child is basically egocentric, while the caregivers, on the other hand, more often see things from others' point of view.

Table 4-15 Subjecthood and modal categories in the caregivers' data and in the child's data

Subjecthood		DY %	DE %	EP %
Self	C	16.4	10.4	8.3
	Q	64.9	29.8	26.3
Others	C	76.1	72.9	37.5
	Q	30.1	57.9	52.6
Neither	C	7.4	16.5	54.1
	Q	5	12.3	21.1

Secondly, most deontic modal utterances had subjects referring to others both in the caregivers' data (73%) and in the child's data (58%). These utterances served to give permission or prohibition to others' actions. For example, 可以玩一小会儿 *kěyǐ wán yī xiǎo huì'er* '(you) can play for a while' (*MOT A 2; 11.27). In comparison with the caregivers (10%), the child (30%) more often produced deontic modal utterances with first person subject 我 *wǒ* 'I'. For example, 我躺可以吧 *wǒ tǎng kěyǐ ba* 'I can lie down, can't I?' (*CHI D 2; 1.07). This suggests the child was more concerned with adults' opinions to her actions.

Thirdly, most epistemic modal utterances had subjects referring to others or neither in both data sets. These utterances were used to describe the speaker's estimation on the likelihood of other's actions or natural occurrences. Such as, 你为什么会流口水啊 *nǐ wèishénme huì liú kǒushuǐ a* 'why would you slaver' (*MOT V 2; 10.01), 妈妈的衣服都要被你给撕坏了 *māma de yīfu dōu yào bèi nǐ gěi sīhuài le* 'mommy's clothes is going to be torn by you' (*MOT V 1; 10.27). The subjects of epistemic modal utterances in the child's data, in comparison, were more frequently used to refer to others and less frequently refer to self or neither. The cause for this difference could be that epistemic modal utterances with subjects referring to others may be cognitive less demanding than those with subjects referring to self or neither.

To sum up, the syntactic structures of modal utterances in the caregivers' data were complex and diverse since period 1, as exemplified by diverse sentence types, complex syntactic structures of subjects, verbs and objects of modal utterances. Those structures in the child's data, however, developed from simple constructions to complex constructions gradually. There exist similarities as well as differences with regard to the relations between sentence types and modal categories in the caregivers' data and those in the child's data. In both data sets, most modals appeared in affirmatives, and deontic modals were more likely to appear in negatives. Caregivers more frequently produced interrogatives than the child did. The interaction style between caregivers and the child, as well as the complex nature of interrogatives may be related to the less frequent occurrences of interrogatives in the child's data. There exist similarities as well as differences with regard to the relations between subjecthood and modal categories in the caregivers' data and those in the child's data. Most subjects of dynamic modal utterances in the caregivers' data referred to others, whereas most those in the child's data referred to the child herself, which may be an illustration of the child's egocentrism. Most subjects of deontic modal utterances in both data sets referred to others, and most subjects of epistemic modal utterances in both data sets referred to others or neither. Apart from those similarities, there also exist differences between the caregivers' data and the child's data on the distribution of subjects of modal utterances.

4.4.4 Summary

The distributional patterns of modal utterances and modal forms in the caregivers' data showed similarities with as well as differences from those in the child's data. Modal utterances in the caregivers' data showed a steady trend of increase from about 5% during period 1 to about 11% during period 8, which agrees with the general trend of increase of modal utterances in the child's data across time periods. Modal utterances were always more frequently occurring in the caregivers' data than in the child's data. The fact that caregivers had been producing modal utterances since period 1 shows that the absence of modal utterances in the child data during period 1 is not related to caregiver input. The general distributional patterns of modal forms in the caregivers' data agree with those in the child's data: frequently occurring modal forms in the caregivers' data tended to be used frequently in the child's data, while infrequently occurring modal forms in the caregivers' data tended to be used infrequently in the child's data. There also exist partial relation between the frequency of caregiver input and the order of acquisition of modals by the child: high frequency of modal forms in the caregivers' input sometimes predicted early modal acquisition.

The distributional patterns of semantic categories of modals in the caregivers' data showed similarities with as well as differences from those in the child's data. Dynamic modals were the most frequently occurring category in the caregivers' data, followed by deontic modals, and epistemic modals were the least frequently occurring category. These distributional patterns agree with those in the child's data, with the exception that dynamic modals accounted for lower percentages in the caregivers' data than those in the child's data, and that deontic and epistemic modals accounted for higher percentages in the caregivers' data than those in the child's data. The distributional patterns of semantic categories of each modal form in both data sets are partially related. Modals 会 *huì* 'know how to, may' and 要 *yào* 'want, must' were mainly dynamic modals in both data sets, while modals 能 *néng* 'can', 可以 *kěyǐ* 'able to, may', 该 *gāi* 'should' and 得 *děi* 'have to, must' were mainly used as a deontic modal in both data sets. Some modal uses in the caregivers' data were not acquired by the child until the end of the investigation, such as the epistemic meaning of modals 能 *néng* 'can' and 得 *děi* 'must'. Frequent modal forms of certain semantic category in the caregivers' data tended to occur frequently in the child's data, while infrequent modal forms of certain semantic category in the caregivers' data tended to occur infrequently in the child's data. The semantics of modals in the caregivers' data showed similarities as well as differences from those in the child's data.

The distributional patterns of syntactic structures in the caregivers' data generally differ from those in the child's data. The sentence types and the syntactic structures of subjects, verbs and objects of modal utterances in the caregivers' data had been diverse from period 1, whereas those in the child's data developed from simple constructions to complex constructions gradually. The relations between sentence types and modal categories in the caregivers' data showed similarities as well as differences from those in the child's data. In both data sets, deontic modals were more likely to occur in negatives. Caregivers were more likely to produce interrogatives than the child, which might be related to the interaction style between caregivers and the child as well as the syntactic complexity involved in interrogatives. The relations between subjecthood and modal categories in the caregivers' data also showed similarities as well as differences from those in the child's data. In both data sets, most deontic modal utterances had subjects referring to others, and most epistemic modal utterances had subjects referring to others or neither. Most dynamic modal utterances in the caregivers' data had subjects referring to others, while most those in the child's data had subjects referring to the child herself. The child's egocentrism and the caregivers' decentration were proposed as the cause of the difference.

Chapter 5

General Discussion

The objective of this chapter is to summarize major findings as well as to discuss the findings within a unified account.

5.1 Summary of Major Findings

The present study investigates the early acquisition of Chinese modals by a single child Q from 1; 4 to 3; 3. Features of modal utterances by her caregivers were also investigated in order to find out to what extent input may affect the acquisition process.

Investigation into the formal, semantic and syntactic aspects of modal uses in the child's data has come to the following findings: modal verbs emerge gradually between the end of 1; 8 and 2; 4, with most modals appearing before 2; 0; dynamic and deontic modals emerge earlier and are more frequently occurring than epistemic modals; modal utterances develop from simple utterances to complex utterances gradually.

Investigation into the formal, semantic and syntactic aspects of modal uses in the caregivers' data has come to the following findings: frequently occurring modals in the caregivers' data tend to be acquired earlier by the child; dynamic and deontic modals are more frequently occurring than epistemic modals; modal utterances are complex since the beginning of the investigation. There only exists partial relation between caregiver input and modal acquisition process by the child.

5.2 Discussion

The aim of this section is to discuss the empirical findings described in chapter 4 with a view to seeking possible answers to research question 5: What factors are at work and how they interact on modal acquisition?

Based on the empirical findings of modal acquisition and theoretical accounts proposed by other researchers, we propose a unified account, a dynamic interactive model of contributing factors to modal acquisition (Figure 5-1), to account for the acquisition process. The basic tenet of the model is that modal acquisition is a gradual process, which is constrained by the dynamic interaction of three factors: linguistic factors, children's cognitive development and caregiver input.

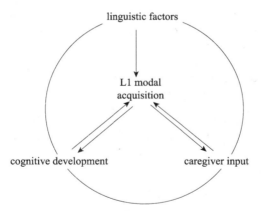

Figure 5-1   A dynamic interactive model of contributing factors on modal acquisition

Linguistic factors, such as linguistic complexity and salience, affect the process of modal acquisition. On the one hand, linguistic complexity of modals may have led to the late acquisition of modals. Literature on L1 modal acquisition converge on the finding that children acquiring different languages start to produce modals around 2; 0, with dynamic and deontic modals acquired earlier than epistemic modals (Wells 1979, 1985; Shepherd 1982, 1993; Stephany 1986; Shatz & Wilcox 1991; Bassano 1996; Papafragou 1998; O'Neill & Atance 2000; the present study). The pattern is partly due to the sematic, pragmatic and syntactic complexity of modals. On the other hand, linguistic salience may facilitate the acquisition of modals. For example, Korean (Choi 1991, 1995) and Japanese (Clancy 1985) sentence-ending suffixes expressing epistemic modal meanings are acquired earlier than English epistemic modals.

The relation between children's cognitive development and modal acquisition is dynamic and bi-directional. On the one hand, the development of modal expressions has often been attributed to the development of underlying cognitive concepts (Gopnik & Astington 1988; Papafragou 1998; Moore, Pure & Furrow 1990; Farrar & Maag 2002; the present study); on the other hand, specific linguistic abilities may actually enhance children's development of theory of mind (Farrar & Maag 2002).

The relation between caregiver input and modal acquisition is dynamic and bi-diretional. On the one hand, caregiver input is partially related to modal acquisition process. Studies have shown that maternal speech has important bearings on modal forms and meanings children learn and use frequently at an early stage (Wells 1979; Shatz & Wilcox 1991; Choi 1991, 1995; Aksu-Koç 1998; the present study); high frequency, however, does not always explain children's early modal development, since children *can* acquire modals that are relatively rarely used by the caregivers (Shatz & Wilcox 1991; Choi 1991, 1995; Aksu-Koç 1998; the present study). On the other hand, modal acquisition process has effect on caregivers' input. Caregivers tend to adjust their input according to the language level of the child. The present study shows that caregivers adjust their input by producing more and more modal utterances with the growing linguistic sophistication of the child.

As has been mentioned in 2.5, previous studies either resort to single factor as explanation for certain aspect of modal acquisition (Perkins 1983; Gopnik & Astington 1988; Papafragou 1998; Moore, Pure & Furrow 1990; Farrar & Maag 2002; Wells 1979; Choi 1991, 1995; etc.), or propose that different factors function at different times in children's modal development (Shatz & Wilcox 1991). Indeed, only when the dynamic interaction of different factors is taken into consideration can we fully explain different aspects of modal acquisition.

Studies of modal acquisition in different languages has shown that modal acquisition starts around 2; 0. Why does modal acquisition start around 2; 0? Why not around 1; 0 when children normally start to produce nouns and verbs referring to concrete objects or actions? It seems that the interaction of linguistic factors with cognitive development has led to the late emergence of modals. As has been discussed in chapter 4, modals are linguistically complex in terms of semantics and syntax. Modals are not like concrete nouns and verbs which refer to concrete objects or actions, like 小狗 xiǎo gǒu 'little doggy' or 走 zǒu 'walk'. Rather, modals refer to abstract notions, like abilities, desires, obligations, possibilities, and so on, which no doubt will put higher demand on the cognitive ability of the child, and will thus be acquired later than those concrete nouns and verbs. Besides, modals are usually placed after subjects and before main verbs, which means only after the subject-verb constructions have been acquired, will modals start to emerge. The present study shows that when the child entered 1; 8, she started to produce subject-verb-object constructions, like 爸爸坐坐 bàba zuòzuo 'daddy sit' (D 1; 8.09), 爸爸开门 bàba kāi mén 'daddy opens the door' (V 1; 8.13), and so on. About 20 days after the acquisition of subject-verb-object constructions, modals started to emerge in the child's speech. Caregiver input seems unrelated to the late emergence of modals, since caregivers produced lots of modal utterances prior to the acquisition of modals. Modal utterances accounted for 5% of total utterances in the caregivers' data during period 1, while modal utterances were non-existent during period 1. The above discussion suggests that input will not become intake until the child is cognitively and linguistically ready to acquire modals.

Studies on modal acquisition all come to the same conclusion that epistemic modals are acquired later than dynamic and deontic modals. The late acquisition of epistemic modals may be the result of the interaction between cognitive development and caregiver input. Since the same modal forms may convey dynamic, deontic as well as epistemic meanings, it would seem difficult to invoke any linguistic reasons for the later appearance of their epistemic uses. Dynamic and deontic modals express the notion of modality in the physical and social world, while epistemic modals function in the mental world and therefore require more effort in cognitive representations. To acquire epistemic modal, children need to realize that beliefs can be different from reality and that beliefs may be held with more or less certainty (Gopnik & Astington 1988; Papafragou 1998; Moore, Pure & Furrow 1990; Farrar & Maag 2002). Besides higher demand on children's theory of mind ability, epistemic modals were also infrequent in the caregivers' input. Epistemic modal utterances accounted for 9% of the total modal utterances in the caregivers' data in the present study. In Shatz and Wilcox's (1991) study, epistemic modals accounted for about 10% of all modal utterances in caregivers' speech. The interaction of high cognitive demand and low caregiver input may have resulted in the late emergence of epistemic modals.

The present study shows that the syntactic structures in the child's data developed from simple constructions to complex constructions gradually. This developmental pattern may be the result of the interaction between linguistic factors and cognitive development. Caregiver input seems unrelated to the above pattern in the child's data. As has been discussed in chapter 4, the syntactic structures of modal utterances in the caregivers' data were diverse from the beginning of the investigation. Various sentence types, as well as complex structures of subjects, verbs, and objects of modal utterances were existent in the caregivers' data since period 1, while those syntactic structures, in contrast, were developing gradually from simple to complex in the child's data. The interaction of linguistic factors with cognitive development seems to be the cause for the syntactic developmental pattern in the child's speech. The first modal utterances in the child's speech were overwhelmingly declaratives, and interrogatives did not emerge until the end of 2; 1. Declaratives are syntactically simpler than interrogatives, which are less cognitive demanding, and thus were acquired earlier by the child. The first modal utterances in the child's data were in the form of bare modals, such as 想 *xiǎng* 'desire', and 会 *huì* 'know how to'. Modal utterances gradually developed to complete utterances with subject, verb and object, such as 妈妈不能吃蛋糕 *māma bù néng chī dàngāo* 'mommy can not eat cake'. Simple utterances are less cognitive demanding than complex utterances, and will therefore be acquired earlier by the child.

References

Aksu-Koç, A. (1998). The role of input vs. universal predispositions in the emergence of tense-aspect morphology: Evidence from Turkish. *First language, 18*, 255-280.

Alleton, V. (1984). *Les auxiliaries de mode en Chinois contemporain*. Paris: Editions de la Maison des Sciences de L'Homme.

Alleton, V. (1994). Some remarks about the epistemic values of auxiliary verbs YINGGAI and YAO in Mandarin Chinese. *Interdisciplinary Studies on Language and Language Change, 1-16*, Pyramid Press.

Austin, J. L. (1962). *How to Do Things with Words*. Oxford: Clarendon Press.

Ba, Jin. (1981). *Jia (Home)*. Beijing: Renmin Wenxue Press.

Bassano, D. (1996). Functional and formal constraints on the emergence of epistemic modality: A longitudinal study on French. *First Language, 16*, 77-113.

Bassano, D., Hickmann, M. & Champaud, C. (1992). Epistemic modality in French children's discourse: 'to be sure' or 'not to be sure'? *Journal of Child Language, 19*: 389-414.

Bates, E. (1976). Pragmatics and sociolinguistics in child language. In D. Morehead and A. Morehead (eds.), *Normal and Deficient Child Language*. Baltimore: University Park Press.

Bi, Shumin. (2012). *Zhuan (Rotation)*. Shijiazhuang: Huashan Wenyi Press.

Bing, Xin. (1983). *Bingxin Wenji 3 (The Collected Works of Bingxin 3)*. Shanghai: Shanghai Wenyi Press.

Bowerman, M. (1986). First steps in acquiring conditionals. In E. C.

Traugott, A. Meulen, J. S. Reilly and C. A. Ferguson (eds.), *On Conditionals* (pp.285-307). Cambridge: Cambridge University Press.

Braunwald, S. R. (1978). Context, word and meaning: Toward a communicational analysis of lexical acquisition. In A. Lock (ed.), *Action, Gesture and Symbol: The Emergence of Language*. London: Academic Press.

Braunwald, S. R. & Brislin, R. W. (1979). The diary method updated. In E. Ochs and B. B. Schieffelin (eds.), *Developmental Pragmatics*. New York: Academic Press.

Brown, R. (1973). *A First Language: The Early Stages*. Cambridge, Massachusetts: Harvard University Press.

Cao, Guilin. (2003). *Beijingren Zai Niuyue (Pekinger in New York)*. Beijing: Zhaohua Press.

CED (1978). *A Chinese-English Dictionary*. Beijing: Commercial Press.

Champaud, C., Bassano, D. & Hickmann, M. (1993). Modalité épistémique et discours rapporté chez l'enfant français. In N. Dittmar and A. Reich (eds.), *Modality in Language Acquisition* (pp.185-210). Berlin/New York: Mouton de Gruyter.

Chao, Y. R. (1968). *A Grammar of Spoken Chinese*. Berkeley: University of California Press.

Choi, S. (1991). Early acquisition of epistemic meanings in Korean: A study of sentence-ending suffixes in the spontaneous speech of three children. *First Language, 11*, 93-119.

Choi, S. (1995). The development of epistemic sentence-ending modal forms and functions in Korean children. In J. Bybee and S. Fleischman (eds.), *Modality in Grammar and Discourse* (pp.165-204). Amsterdam: Benjamins.

Choi, S. (2006). Acquisition of modality. In W. Frawley (ed.), *The Expression of Modality* (pp.141-171). Berlin: Mouton de Gruyter.

Chomsky, N. (1957). *Syntactic Structures*. The Hague: Mouton.

Clancy, P. (1985). The acquisition of Japanese. In D. I. Slobin (ed.), *The Crosslinguistic Study of Language Acquisition, vol. 1* (pp.373-524). Hillsdale: Lawrence Erlbaum Associates.

Clark, R. (1982). Theory and method in child-language research: Are we assuming too much? In S. A. Kuczaj (ed.), *Language development. Vol. I. Syntax and semantics*. Hillsdale, New Jersey: Lawrence Erlbaum.

Coates, J. (1983). *The Semantics of the Modal Auxiliaries*. London and Canberra: Croom Helm.

Coates, J. (1988). The acquisition of the meaning of modality in children aged eight and twelve. *Journal of Child Language, 15,* 425-434.

Creswell, J. (1998). *Qualitative Inquiry and Research Design: Choosing Among Five Traditions*. Thousand Oaks, CA: Sage.

Ding, Shengshu, Lü, Shuxiang & Li, Rong, et al. (1953). Yüfa Jianghua (Some remarks about Chinese grammar) (9). *Zhongguo Yüwen (Journal of Chinese Language), 3,* 26-29.

Dromi, E. (1987). *Early Lexical Development*. Cambridge: Cambridge University Press.

Duff, P. (2008). *Case Study Research in Applied Linguistics*. New York: Lawrence Erlbaum Associates.

Erbaugh, M. (1982). *Coming to order: Natural selection and the origin of syntax in the Chinese-speaking child* (Unpublished doctoral dissertation). University of California, Berkeley.

Fan, Xiao, Du, Gaoyin & Chen, Guanglei. (1987). *Hanyü Dongci Gaishu (On Chinese Verbs)*. Shanghai: Shanghai Foreign Language Education Press.

Farrar, M. J. & Maag, L. (2002). Early language development and the emergence of a theory of mind. *First Language, 22,* 197-213.

Fenson, L., Dale, P., Reznick, J. S., et al. (1993). *MacArthur Communicative Development Inventories: User's Guide and Technical*

Manual. San Diego, CA: Singular Publishing Group.

Fletcher, P. (1978). The development of the verb-phrase. In P. Fletcher & M. Garman (eds). *Language Acquisition* (pp.261-284). Cambridge: Cambridge University Press.

Forguson, L. & Gopnik, A. (1988). The ontogeny of common sense. In J. Astington, P. Harris & D. Olson (eds.), *Developing theories of mind* (pp.226-243). New York: Cambridge University Press.

Gao, Mingkai. (1948). *Hanyü Yüfa Lun (On Chinese Grammar).* Shanghai: Kaiming Bookstore. Rpt. By Beijing: Commercial Press, 1986.

Garcia, E. (1976). Auxiliaries and the criterion of simplicity. *Language, 43,* 853-870.

Gee, J. & Savasir, I. (1985). On the use of will and gonna: Toward a description of activity-types for child language. *Discourse Processes, 8,* 143-175.

Gerhardt, J. (1991). The meaning and use of the modals *hafta, needta,* and *wanna* in children's speech. *Journal of Pragmatics, 16,* 531-590.

Gerring, J. (2001). *Social Science Methodology: A Criterial Framework.* Cambridge: Cambridge University Press.

Gleason, J. B. (2005). *The Development of Language.* Beijing: Beijing World Publishing Corporation.

Gopnik, A. & Astington, J. (1988). Children's understanding of representational change in its relation to the understanding of false belief and the appearance-reality distinction. *Child Development, 59,* 26-37.

Guba, E. G. & Lincoln, Y. S. (1981). *Effective Evaluation.* San Francisco: Jossy Bass.

Guo, J. S. (1994). *Social interaction, meaning, and grammatical form: Children's development and use of modal auxiliaries in Mandarin Chinese* (Unpublished doctoral dissertation). University of California, Berkeley.

Halliday, M. A. K. (1973). *Explorations in the Functions of Language.*

London: Edward Arnold.

Halliday, M. A. K. (1975). *Learning How to Mean: Explorations in the Development of Language*. London: Edward Arnold.

He, Rong. (1942). *Zhongguo Wenfa Lun (On Chinese Grammar)*. Independence Press. Rpt. By Beijing: Commercial Press, 1985.

Hirst, W. & Weil, J. (1982). Acquisition of epistemic and deontic meaning of modality. *Journal of Child Language, 9*, 659-666.

Hoff-Ginsberg, E. & Shatz, M. (1982). Linguistic input and the child's acquisition of modals. *Journal of Child Language, 9*, 115-124.

Hu, Yüshu & Fan, Xiao. (1995). *Dongci Yanjiu (Studies of Verbs)*. Kaifeng: *Henan University Press*.

Huddleston, R. D. (1976). Some theoretical issues in the description of the English verb. *Lingua 40*, 331-383.

Ji, Yixin. (1986). Yingyü Qingtai Zhudongci Yü Hanyü néngyuàn Dongci De Bijiao (Comparison between English modal auxiliaries and Chinese Nengyuan verbs). *Yüyan Jiaoxue Yü Yanjiu (Language Teaching and Research), 3*, 76-77.

Johnson, D. M. (1992). *Approaches to Research in Second Language Learning*. New York: Longman.

Kuczaj, S. & Daly, M. (1979). The development of hypothetical reference in the speech of young children. *Journal of Child Language, 6*, 563-579.

Kuczaj, S. & Maratsos, M. (1983). Initial verbs of yes-no questions: A different kind of general grammatical category. *Developmental Psychology, 19*, 440-444.

Lao, She. (1957). Liujia Dayuan (Lius' Yard). Included in *Laoshe Duanpian Xiaoshuo Xuan (Laoshe Short Stories)*. Beijing：Renmin Wenxue Press.

Lao, She. (2012). *Sishi Tong Tang (The Yellow Storm)*. Beijing: Beijing Shiyue Wenyi Press. 老舍. 2012.

Larsen-Freeman, D. (1997). Chaos/complexity science and second language acquisition. *Applied Linguistics, 18,* 141-165.

Leslie, A. & Thaiss, L. (1992). Domain specificity in conceptual development. *Cognition, 43,* 225-251.

Li, C. N. & Thompson, S. A. (1981). *Mandarin Chinese: A Functional Reference Grammar.* Berkeley: University of California Press.

Li, Jinxi. (1924). *Xinzhu Guoyü Wenfa (A New Grammar of Chinese Language).* Shanghai: Commercial Press. Rpt. by Beijing: Commercial Press, 1992.

Li, Linding. (1986). *Xiandai Hanyü Jüxing (Sentence Patterns in Modern Chinese).* Beijing: Commercial Press.

Li, R. Z. (2003). *Modality in English and Chinese: A typically perspective* (Unpublished doctoral dissertation). University of Antwerp.

Lieven, E., Behrens, H., Spears, J., et al. (2003). Early syntactic creativity: A usage-based approach. *Journal of Child Language, 30,* 333-370.

Lincoln, Y. & Guba, E. G. (1985). *Naturalistic Inquiry.* Beverly Hills: Sage.

Liu, Yuehua, Pan, Wenyü & Gu, Wei. (1983). *Shiyong Xiandai Hanyü Yüfa (Practical Modern Chinese Grammar).* Beijing: Foreign Language Teaching & Research Press.

Lu, Jingwen. (1991). *Hanying Yüfa Bijiao (Chinese-English Grammatical Comparison).* Shanxi Education Press.

Lü, Shuxiang. (1942). *Zhongguo Wenfa Yaolue (Outlines of Chinese Grammar).* Shanghai: Commercial Press. Rpt. by Beijing: Commercial Press, 1982.

Lü, Shuxiang. (1985). Yiwen、Fouding、Kending (Interrogatives, Negatives, Positives). *Zhongguo Yüwen (Journal of Chinese language), 4,* 241-250.

Lü, Shuxiang, Li, Linding & Liu, Jian, et al. (1980). *Xiandai Hanyü Babai Ci (Eight Hundred Words in Modern Chinese).* Hong Kong: Commercial Press.

Ma, Jianzhong. (1898). *Mashi Wentong (Ma's Grammar).* Shanghai:

Commercial Press. Rpt. by Beijing: Commercial Press, 1983.

MacWhinney, B. (2009). *The CHAT Transcription Format.* http://childes. psy. cmu.edu/manuals/chat.pdf.

Merriam, S. (1998). *Qualitative Research and Case Study Applications in Education* (2nd edn.). San Francisco: Jossey-Bass.

Mervis, C., Mervis, C. & Johnson, K., et al. (1992). Early lexical development: The value of the diary method. In C. Rovee-Collier & L. Lipsett (eds.), *Advances in Infancy Research* (Vol. 8). Norwood, NJ: Ablex.

Miles, M. and Huberman, A. M. (1994). *Qualitative Data Analysis* (2nd edn.). Thousand Oaks, CA: Sage.

Moore, C., Pure, K. & Furrow, D. (1990). Children's understanding of the modal expression of speaker certainty and uncertainty and its relation to the development of a representational theory of mind. *Child Development, 61*: 722-730.

Müller, N. (1998). Transfer in bilingual first language acquisition. *Bilingualism: Language and Cognition, 3*, 151-171.

Nelson, K. & Lucariello, J. (1985). The development of meaning in first words. In M. Barrett (ed.), *Children's single-word speech*. New York: Wiley.

Nunan, D. (1992). *Research Methods in Language Learning*. Cambridge: Cambridge University Press.

Nuyts, J. (2006). Modality: Overview and linguistic issues. In W. Frawley (ed.), *The Expression of Modality* (pp.1-26). Berlin: Mouton.

O'Neill, D. & Atance, C. (2000). "Maybe my daddy gives me a big piano": The development of children's use of modals to express uncertainty. *First Language, 20*, 29-52.

Palmer, F. R. (1979). *Modality and the English Modality*. London: Longman Ltd.

Palmer, F. R. (1986). *Mood and Modality*. Cambridge: Cambridge University Press.

Palmer, F. R. (1990) *Modality and the English Modals* (2nd edn.). London: Longman.

Papafragou, A. (1998). The acquisition of modality: Implications for theories of semantic representation. *Mind and Language, 13*, 370-99.

Papafragou, A. (2000). *Modality: Issues in the Semantics-pragmatics Interface*. Oxford: Elsevier Science Ltd.

Pea, R. & Mawby, R. (1984). Semantics of modal auxiliary verb uses by preschool children. *Proceedings of the International Congress for the Study of Child Language, 2*: 204-219.

Peng, Lizhen. (2005). *Xiandai Hanyü Qingtai Yanjiu (Studies on Modern Chinese Modality)*. Unpublished Ph.D. Dissertation, Fudan University.

Perkins, M. R. (1983). *Modal Expressions in English*. London: Frances Pinter.

Peters, A. (1983). *The Units of Language Acquisition*. Cambridge: Cambridge University Press.

Piaget, J. (1965). *Moral Judgment of the Child*. New York: Free Press.

Premack, D. & Woodruff, G. (1978). Does the chimpanzee have a theory of mind? *Behavioral and Brain Sciences, 1*, 515-526.

Quirk, R., Greenbaum, S., Leech, G., et al. (1985). *A Comprehensive Grammar of the English Language*. London: Longman.

Rist, C. A. (1977). On the relation among educational research paradigms: From disdain to détente. *Anthropology and Education Quarterly, 8*, 42-49.

Rodgon, M. (1976). *Single Word Usage, Cognitive Development, and the Beginnings of Combinatorial Speech: A Study of Ten English-speaking Children*. Cambridge: Cambridge University Press.

Shallice, J. (1979). Case study approach in neuropsychological research. *Journal of Clinical Neuropsychology, 1*, 183-211.

Shatz, M., Billman, D. & Yaniv, I. (1986). *Early Occurrences of English Auxiliaries in Children's Speech. Unpublished manuscript*. Ann Arbor: University of Michigan.

Shatz, M., Grimm, H., Wilcox, S., et al. (1990). *Modal Expressions in German and American Mother-Child Conversations: Implications for Input Theories of Language Acquisition* (Unpublished manuscript). University of Michigan, Ann Arbor.

Shatz, M., Hoff-Ginsberg, E. & MacIver, D. (1989). Induction and the acquisition of English auxiliaries: The effects of differentially enriched input. *Journal of Child Language, 16*, 121-140.

Shatz, M. & Wilcox, S. (1991). Constraints on the acquisition of English modality. In S. Gelman & J. Byrnes (eds.), *Perspectives on Language and Thought* (pp.319-353). Cambridge: Cambridge University Press.

Shaughnessy, J. J. & Zechmeister, E. B. (1985). *Research Methods in Psychology*. New York: Alfred A. Knopf.

Shepherd, S. (1982). From deontic to epistemic: An analysis of modality in the history of English, creoles, and language acquisition. In A. Ahlqvist (ed.), *Papers from the 5th International Conference on Historical Linguistics* (pp.123-316). Amsterdam: Benjamins.

Shepherd, S. (1993). The acquisition of modality in Antiguan Creole. In N. Dittmar & A. Reich (eds.), *Modality in Language Acquisition* (pp.171- 184). Berlin: De Gruyter.

Slobin, D. I. (1985). Cross-linguistic evidence for the language-making capacity. In D. I. Slobin (ed.), *The Crosslinguistic Study of Language Acquisition. Vol. 2: Theoretical Issues* (pp. 1157-1256). Hillsdale, NJ: Lawrence Erlbaum Associates.

Smoczynska, M. (1993). The acquisition of Polish modal verbs. In N. Dittmar and A. Reich (eds.), *Modality in Language Acquisition* (pp.145-170). Berlin/New York: Mouton de Gruyter.

Stake, R. E. (1978). The case study method in social inquiry. *Educational Researcher, 7*, 5-8.

Stake, R. E.(1981). Case study methodology: An Epistemological advocacy.

In W. W. Wlesh (ed.), *Case Study Methodology in Educational Evaluation.* Proceedings of the 1981 Minnesota Educational Conference. Minneapolis: Minnesota Research and Evaluation Center.

Stephany, U. (1979). *The modality constituent— a neglected area in the studies of first language acquisition.* Köln: Inst. für Sprachwiss.

Stephany, U. (1986). Modality. In P. Fletcher & M. Garman (eds.), *Language Acquisition* (pp.375-400). Cambridge: Cambridge University Press.

Stephany, U. (1993). Modality in first language acquisition: The state of the art. In N. Dittmar & A. Reich (eds.), *Modality in Language Acquisition.* Berlin: De Gruyter.

Stern, C. & Stern, W. (1928/1975). *Die Kindersprache.* Darmstadt: Wissens- chaftliche Buchgesellschaft.

Tardif, T. (1996). Nouns are not always learned before verbs: Evidence from Mandarin speakers' early vocabularies. *Developmental Psychology, 32,* 492-504.

Tardif, T., Fletcher, P., Linang, W. L., et al. (2002, July). Nouns and verbs in children's early vocabularies: A cross-linguistic study of the MacArthur Communicative Development Inventory in English, Mandarin, and Cantonese. Poster session at joint conference of International Association for the Study of Child Language and Society for Research in Communication Disorder. Madison, Wisconsin.

Tardif, T. & Fu, X. (in preparation). *Does what you say influence what you remember? Nouns and verbs in English and Mandarin Chinese* (Unpublished manuscript). University of Michigan.

Tardif, T., Gelman, S. A. & Xu, F. (1999). Putting the "noun bias" in context: A comparision of English and Mandarin. *Child Development, 70,* 620-635.

Tardif, T., Shatz, M. & Naigles, L. (1997). Caregiver speech and children's use of nouns versus verbs: A comparison of English, Italian, and Mandarin. *Journal of Child Language, 24,* 535-565.

Tomasello, M. (1992). *First Verbs: A Case Study of Early Grammatical Development.* Cambridge: Cambridge University Press.

Tomasello, M. (2003). *Constructing a Language: A Usage-based Theory of Language Acquisition.* Cambridge, Massachusetts: Harvard University Press.

Torr, J. (1998). The development of modality in the pre-school years: Language as a vehicle for understanding possibilities and obligations in everyday life. *Functions of Language, 5,* 157-178.

Tsang, Chui-lim. (1981). *A semantic study of modal auxiliary verbs in Chinese (Unpublished doctoral dissertation).* Stanford University.

Ungerer, F. & Schmid, H-J. (1996). *An Introduction to Cognitive Linguistics.* London & New York: Longman.

van Lier, L. (1997). Observation from an ecological perceptive. *TESOL Quarterly, 22,* 783-787.

van Lier, L. (2004). *The Ecology and Semiotics of Language Learning: A Sociocultural Perspective.* Heidelberg: Kluwer Academic.

Wang, Li. (1943). *Zhongguo Xiandai Yüfa (Modern Chinese Grammar).* Shanghai: Commercial Press. Rpt. by Beijing: Commercial Press, 1985.

Wang, Li. (1944). *Zhongguo Yüfa Lilun (Theory of Chinese Grammar).* Shanghai: Commercial Press. Rpt. by Jinan: Shandong Education Press, 1984.

Wang, Shaoxin. (1985). "De" Zi De Yüyi、Yüfa Zuoyong Yanbian (Development of dé in meaning and grammatical functions). *Yüwen Yanjiu (Chinese Studies), 1:* 43-49.

Wellman, H. (1990). *The Child's Theory of Mind.* Massachusetts: The MIT Press.

Wells, G. (1979). Learning and using the auxiliary verb in English. In V. Lee (ed.), *Cognitive Development: Language and Thinking From*

Birth to Adolescence (pp.250-270). London: Croom Helm.

Wells, G. (1985). *Language Development in the Preschool Years.* Cambridge: Cambridge University Press.

Wimmer, H. & Perner, J. (1983). Beliefs about beliefs: Representation and constraining function of wrong beliefs in young children's understanding of deception. *Cognition, 13,* 103-128.

Yin, R. (2003). *Case Study Research: Design and Methods.* Thousand Oaks, California: Sage.

Yip, P. & Rimmingtong, D. (1997). *Chinese: An Essential Grammar.* London: Routledge.

Zaitchik, D. (1990). When representations conflict with reality: The preschooler's problem with false beliefs and "false" photographs. *Cognition, 35,* 41-68.

Zhongguo Shehui Kexueyuan Yüyan Yanjiusuo Cidian Bianjishi. (1998). *Xiandai Hanyü Cidian (A Modern Chinese Dictionary).* Beijing: Commercial Press.

Zhu, Dexi. (1982). *Yüfa Jiangyi (Lecture Notes on Chinese Grammar).* Beijing: Commercial Press.

The First Five Occurrences of Modals in the Child's Data

1. 想 *xiǎng*

The first five dynamic 想 *xiǎng* 'desire' utterances

i. (The child is looking at a picture of horse.) V 1; 8.27

*FAT: 想　　不　　想　　骑　马　　　呀?
    Xiǎng bù xiǎng qí mǎ ya?
    desire not desire ride horse P
    'Do you want to ride a horse or not?'

*CHI: 想。
    Xiǎng.
    desire
    '(I) want to (ride a horse).'

ii. (The child is drawing with a pen.) V 1; 9.10

*FAT: 你　　想　　　不　想　　玩　　娃娃?
    Nǐ xiǎng bù xiǎng wán wáwa?
    you desire not desire play doll
    'Do you want to play with the doll or not?'

*CHI: 不　　想。
    Bù xiǎng.
    not desire
    '(I) do not want to (play with the doll).'

iii. (The child is playing by herself.) V 1; 9.10

*FAT: 你　　想　　不　想　　吃　橘子?

　　　　Nǐ　　xiǎng　　bù　xiǎng　　chī　júzi?

　　　　you　　desire　　not　desire　　eat　orange

　　　　'Do you want to have an orange or not?'

*CHI: 不　　想。

　　　　Bù　　xiǎng.

　　　　not　　desire

　　　　'(I) do not want to (have an orange).'

iv. (The child is playing by herself.) V 1; 9.10

*FAT: 想　　不　想　　给　　婆婆　　打　电话　　啊?

　　　　Xiǎng bù　xiǎng　gěi　pópo　dǎ　diànhuà　a?

　　　　desire not　desire　give grandma call　phone　P

　　　　'Do you want to give grandma a phone call or not?'

*CHI: 不　　想。

　　　　Bù　　xiǎng.

　　　　not　　desire

　　　　'(I) do not want to (give grandma a phone call).'

v. (The child is playing by herself.) V 1; 9.10

*FAT: 你　　想　　不　想　　给　　妈妈　　打　电话?

　　　　Nǐ　　xiǎng bù　xiǎng　gěi　māma　dǎ　diànhuà?

　　　　you　　desire not　desire　give　mommy call　phone

　　　　'Do you want to give mommy a phone call or not?'

*CHI: 不　　想。

　　　　Bù　　xiǎng.

　　　　not　　desire

　　　　'(I) do not want to (give mommy a phone call).'

2. 会 *huì*

The first five dynamic 会 *huì* 'know how to' utterances

i. & ii. (The child tries to turn on the DVD to listen to music.) D 1; 8.29

> *GRF: 你　　会　　不　　会?
> Nǐ　　huì　　bú　　huì?
> you　　can　　not　　can
> 'Can you (turn on the DVD)?'
> *CHI: 会。
> Huì.
> can
> '(I) can (turn on the DVD).'
> *GRF: 0.
> %act: 帮芊芊打开 DVD (turning on DVD for the child)
> *CHI: 爸爸　　会。
> Bàba　　huì.
> daddy　can
> 'Daddy can (turn on the DVD)'
> %act: 拍着 DVD　　(patting on the DVD)

iii. (Grandpa helps the child to put on her shoes, while she insists on doing that by herself.) D 1; 8.30

> *GRF: 你　　自己　　会　穿　　吗?
> Nǐ　　zìjǐ　　huì　chuān　　ma?
> you　　yourself　can　put on　　P
> 'Can you put (the shoes) on by yourself?'
> *CHI: 会。
> Huì.
> can
> '(I) can (put on the shoes by myself).'

iv. & v. (The child saw daddy taking notes.) D 1; 9.06

*CHI: 爸爸　　会　　写字。

Bàba　　huì　　xiězì.

daddy　can　　write

'Daddy can write.'

*GRM: 爸爸　会　　写字,　你　会　不　会?

Bāba　huì　　xiězì,　nǐ　huì　bú　huì?

daddy can　　write　you can not can

'Daddy can　write. Can you?'

*CHI: 会。

Huì.

can

'(I) can (write).'

3. 要 yào

The first five deontic 要 yào 'must' utterances

i. (Mommy is taking notes, while Q wants mommy to take her out.) D 1; 9.23

*CHI: 妈妈　　　不　　要　　写。

Māma　　bú　yào　xiě.

mommy　not　must　write

'Do not write, mommy.'

ii. (Q is building lego, while daddy keeps tickling her feet.) V 1; 11.22

*CHI: 不　　要。

Bú　yào.

not　must

'Do not (tickle me, daddy).'

iii. (Aunt kicked Q's toy goose by accident.) D 2; 0.16

*CHI: 不　要　　踢　我　鹅。

Bú　yào　tī　wǒ　é.

not　must　kick　my　goose

'Do not kick my goose (aunt).'

iv. (Grandpa is coming over when Q is playing in mom's room.) D 2; 1.22

*CHI: 爷爷　　　不　要　　过来。

Yéye　　bú　yào　guòlai.

grandpa　not　must　come over

'Do not come over, grandpa.'

v. (Q wants to play with a little cat on the road, but the cat is scared away.) D 2; 2.18

*CHI: 不　要　　跑。

Bú　yào　pǎo.

not　must　run

'Do not run away (little cat).'

The first five dynamic modal 要 yào 'want' utterances

i. (Daddy is going to build Qian Qian's lego.) V 1; 11.22

*CHI: 芊芊　　　要　玩。

Qiān Qian　yào　wán.

Qian Qian　want　play

'I want to build the lego.'

ii. (Qian Qian is ready to throw a doll into the air.) V 1; 11.22

*CHI: 芊芊　　　要　扔　　高。

Qiān Qian　yào　rēng　gāo.

Qian Qian　want　throw　high

'Qian Qian want to throw this into the air.'

iii. (It is raining. Q reaches out her hand into the rain while standing on the balcony.) V 2; 0.13

*CHI: 我　要　　洗　手。

    Wǒ   yào   xǐ   shǒu.

    I   want   wash hand

    'I want to wash my hand.'

iv. (Q is drawing.) D 2; 0.30

*CHI: 我　要　　洗澡。

    Wǒ   yào   xǐzǎo.

    I   want   take a bath

    'I want to take a bath.'

v. (Mommy is going to unwrap a zongzi for Qian Qian.) D 2; 1.12

*CHI: 我　　要　　　剥剥。

    Wǒ   yào   bōbo.

    I   want   unwrap

    'I want to unwrap the zongzi.'

The first five epistemic modal 要 *yào* 'must' utterances

i. (Qian Qian saw her aunt standing on the edge of the bed tucking in the mosquito net) D 2; 1.19

*CHI: 姑姑　要　　摔倒　　　了。

    Gūgu   yào   shuāidǎo   le.

    aunt   will   fall down   PHA

    'Aunt is falling down.'

ii. (Qian Qian is playing with Yuan Yuan while Yuan Yuan's grandma tells her to go back home) D 2; 1.22

*CHI: 圆圆　　　要　　回家　　　了。

    Yuán Yuan   yào   huíjiā   le.

    Yuan Yuan   about to   go back home   PHA

    'Yuan Yuan is going back home.'

iii. (Qian Qian saw grandpa standing at the doorway fully dressed up.) D 2; 1.26

*CHI: 姥爷　　　要　　　出去　　　了。
　　　Lǎoye　　yào　　chūqù　　le.
　　　grandpa　about to go out　PHA
　　　'Grandpa is going out.'

iv. (Qian Qian saw a boy walking towards the door of the playground.) D 2; 1.28

*CHI: 哥哥　　　要　　　出去　　　了。
　　　Gēge　　yào　　chūqù　　le.
　　　brother　about to　go out　PHA
　　　'The brother is getting out.'

v. (Qian Qian saw a puppy trying to jump down from the top of its cage) D 2; 1.28

*CHI: 汪汪　　　要　　　掉　　下去　　了。
　　　Wāngwang　yào　　diào　xiàqu　le.
　　　dog　　　about to　fall　down　PHA
　　　'The dog is falling down.'

4. 敢 *gǎn*

The first five dynamic modal 敢 *gǎn* 'dare' utterances

i. (Mommy is drinking Chinese medicine, and invites the child to taste it. The child refuses to do that) D 1; 9.25

*MOT: 敢　不　敢　尝?
　　　Gǎn　bù　gǎn　cháng?
　　　dare　not　dare　taste
　　　'Do you dare to taste it?'
*CHI: 不　　敢　　尝。
　　　Bù　　gǎn　　cháng.

not   dare   taste

'(I) dare not taste (it).'

*MOT: 那   好,   妈妈   喝   药。

Nà   hǎo,   māma   hē   yào.

then   all right   mommy   drink   medicine

'Then all right. Mommy will drink the medicine.'

*CHI: 芊芊   看看   妈妈   喝。

Qiān Qian   kànkan   māma   hē.

Qian Qian   watch   mommy   drink

'Qian Qian will watch mommy drinking.'

ii. (Something was wrong with the door. Mommy stuck a piece of adhesive plaster on the door.) D 1; 11.12

*CHI: 芊芊   不   贴。

Qiān Qian   bù   tiē.

Qian Qian   not   stick

'Qian Qian will not be stuck (with the adhesive plaster). '

*CHI: 门   贴。

Mén   tiē.

door   stick

'The door will be stuck (with the adhesive plaster).'

*CHI: 妈妈   害   疼。

Māma   hài   téng.

mommy   afraid   pain

'Mommy is afraid of pain.'

*CHI: 不   敢   贴。

Bù   gǎn   tiē.

not   dare   stick

'Not dare to stick (the adhesive plaster on her).'

iii. & iv. (In the morning, the child just gets up) D 1; 11.20

*CHI: 坐   鸵鸟。

> Zuò   tuóniǎo.
> sit   ostrich
> '(To) sit on an ostrich.'

*CHI: 芊芊   不   敢。

> Qiān Qian   bù   gǎn.
> Qian Qian   not   dare
> 'Qian Qian dare not (to sit on an ostrich).'

*MOT: 妈妈   敢。

> Māma   gǎn.
> mommy   dare
> 'Mommy dare (to sit on an ostrich).'

@Comment: 大概想起来动物园的事儿了(The child probably has recalled the occurrences at the zoo.)

v. (Daddy grabs the child's cup and intends to drink water from it) D 2; 0.11

*CHI: 辣。

> Là.
> hot
> '(It is) hot.'

*CHI: 爸爸   不   敢   喝。

> Bàba   bù   gǎn   hē.
> daddy   not   dare   drink
> 'Daddy dare not drink it.'

*CHI: 辣椒。

> Làjiāo.
> cayenne
> '(It is) cayenne.'

*FAT: 爸爸   不   怕   辣。

> Bàba   bú   pà   là.
> daddy   not   afraid   hot
> 'Daddy is not afraid of hot (food).'

*CHI: 爸爸　　怕　　辣　　的。
   Bàba pà là de.
   daddy afraid hot EMP
   'Daddy is afraid of hot (food).'

*CHI: 爸爸　　不　　敢　　喝。
   Bàba bù gǎn hē.
   daddy not dare drink
   'Daddy dare not drink (it).'

@Comment: 说水辣是为了阻止爸爸喝她水杯里的水 (The child says the water is hot in order to prevent daddy from drinking water from her cup)

5. 用 *yòng*

The first five deontic modal 用 *yòng* 'need' utterances

i. & ii. (Mommy took the child home from outside. The child insists on holding mommy's hands inside the house.) D 1; 9.28

*MOT: 屋里　　不　　用　　扯。
   Wūlǐ bú yòng chě.
   inside not need hold
   'There is no need to hold (hands) inside.'

*CHI: 用　　吧。
   Yòng ba.
   need P
   'There is need (to hold hands inside).'

*CHI: 用。
   Yòng.
   need
   'There is need to (hold hands inside).'

iii. & iv. (Mommy rubs the child's arms while bathing her) D 2; 1.10

*CHI: 不　　用　　搓　　胳膊。

      Bú　yòng　cuō　gēbo.

      not　need　rub　arm

      'There is no need to rub the arms.'

*CHI: 不　　用　　搓　　腿。

      Bú　yòng　cuō　tuǐ.

      not　need　rub　legs

      'There is no need to rub the legs.'

v. (Mommy intends to change clothes for the child) D 2; 2.09

*MOT: 妈妈　　给　你　　换换　　衣服　　吧?

       Māma　gěi　nǐ　huànhuan　yīfu　ba?

       mommy　for　you　change　clothes　P

       'Shall mommy change clothes for you?'

*MOT: 你　穿　　得　太　热。

       Nǐ　chuān　de　tài　rè.

       you　wear　P　too　hot

       'You are wearing too much.'

*CHI: 不　　用　　换。

      Bú　yòng　huàn.

      not　need　change

      'There is no need to change (my clothes).'

*CHI: 不　　用　　换。

      Bú　yòng　huàn.

      not　need　change

      'There is no need to change (my clothes)'.

The first five dynamic modal 用 *yòng* 'need' utterances

i. (One of the child's shoe falls off, and the child put it on by herself) D 2; 3.11

*CHI: 我　　会 穿　　鞋　　了。

      Wǒ　huì chuān　xié　le.

I   can put on shoe PHA

'I can put on shoes.'

*CHI: 不   用   妈妈   帮   了。

Bú   yòng māma   bāng le.

not   need mommy help   PHA

'(I) do not need mommy to help (me) any more.'

ii. & iii. (The child is sitting on the swing. Mommy pushes her to help her swing higher) D 2; 3.13

*CHI: 不   用   扶。

Bú   yòng fú.

not   need hold

'(I) do not need (you) to hold (me).'

*CHI: 不   用   推。

Bú   yòng tuī.

not   need push

'(I) do not need (you) to push (me).'

iv. (The child asks mommy to help her with her drawing, whereas mommy refuses to do that.) D 2; 10.11

*CHI: 我   不   用   帮忙   也   可以   的。

Wǒ   bú   yòng bāngmáng yě   kěyǐ   de.

I   not   need   help   also   may   EMP

'I can do it without (your) help.'

v. (Mommy asks the child to take some pills) D 3; 0.21

*CHI: 我   不   用   塞   xx, 就   能   咽   下去。

Wǒ   bú   yòng sāi xx, jiù   néng yàn   xiàqù.

I   not   need plug xx CONJ can swallow down

'I can swallow (the pills) without plugging xx.'

6. 愿意 *yuànyì*

The first five dynamic modal 愿意 *yuànyì* 'willing' utterances

i. (The child is playing at home with her family) V 1; 10.04

*MOT: 芊芊 跟 弟弟 妹妹 玩儿。

   Qiān Qian gēn dìdi mèimei wán'er.

   Qian Qian with brother sister play

   'Qian Qian will play with brother and sister.'

@Comment: 弟弟妹妹指的是芊芊的玩具 (Brother and sister here refer to the child's dolls.)

*FAT: 愿意 不 愿意?

   Yuànyì bú yuànyì.

   willing not willing

   'Are you willing or not (to play with brother and sister)?'

*CHI: 愿意。

   Yuànyì.

   willing

   '(I'm) willing (to play with brother and sister).'

*FAT: 想 不 想?

   Xiǎng bù xiǎng.

   desire not desire

   'Do you want (to play with brother and sister)?'

*CHI: 想。

   Xiǎng.

   desire

   '(I) want to (play with brother and sister).'

*GRM: 愿意 举   手。

   Yuànyì jǔ   shǒu.

   willing raise up hand

   '(If) you are willing (to play with brother and sister), (then) raise up your hand.'

*CHI: 0.

%act: 举起一只手 (raising up one hand)

ii. & iii (The child is playing with her father) D 1; 11.29

*FAT: 爸爸 　带 　芊芊 　坐 飞机 　吧?

　　　　Bàba 　*dài* 　*QiānQian* 　*zuò fēijī* 　*ba?*

　　　　daddy take 　QianQian sit plane 　P

　　　　'Daddy take Qian Qian (to go somewhere) by plane?'

*CHI: 坐 　大象。

　　　　Zuò 　*dàxiàng.*

　　　　sit 　elephant

　　　　'(I want to) sit on an elephant.'

*CHI: 坐 　鸵鸟。

　　　　Zuò 　*tuóniǎo.*

　　　　sit 　ostrich

　　　　'(I want to) sit on an ostrich.'

*FAT: 坐 　大象 　得 　去 　泰国。

　　　　Zuò 　*dàxiàng* 　*děi* 　*qù* 　*tàiguó.*

　　　　sit 　elephant 　have to 　go to 　Tailand

　　　　'(You) have to go to Tailand to sit on an elephant.'

*CHI: 愿意 　让 芊芊 　坐。

　　　　Yuànyì 　*ràng* 　*Qiān Qian* 　*zuò.*

　　　　willing 　let 　Qian Qian 　sit

　　　　'(The elephant is) willing to let Qian Qian sit (on it).'

*FAT: 0.

%act: 抱芊芊去厕所尿尿 (taking the child to the bathroom to pee)

*CHI: 大象 　不 愿 　让 　芊芊 　坐。

　　　　Dàxiàng 　*bú* 　*yuàn* 　*ràng* 　*QiānQian* 　*zuò.*

　　　　elephant 　not 　willing 　let 　QianQian 　sit

　　　　'The elephant is not willing to let QianQian sit (on it).'

*FAT: 芊芊 　乖 的话大象 　就 让 乖乖 芊芊 　坐。

　　　　QiānQian guāi dehuà dàxiàng jiù ràng guāiguai QiānQian zuò.

QianQian good then elephant CONJ let good QianQian sit
'(If) Qian Qian is good, (then) the elephant will let good baby sit (on it).'

iv. (Mommy washed some fruits for the child.) D 2; 3.13

*GRM: 你　　得　　　问问　　芊芊　　愿　　不愿意吃。
　　　Nǐ　　děi　　wènwen　QiānQiān　yuàn　bú yuànyì chī.
　　　you　have to　ask　　QianQian willing not willing eat
　　　'You have to ask QianQian whether she wants to have these or not.'

%add: MOT
*CHI: 愿意　　　　吃。
　　　Yuànyi　　chī.
　　　willing　　eat
　　　'(I'm) willing (to have these fruits).'

v. (The child is walking towards the balcony.) D 2; 5.25

*GRF: 芊芊　　　你　　干　　什么?
　　　Qiān Qian　nǐ　gàn　shénme?
　　　Qian Qian　you　do　what
　　　'What are you going to do, Qian Qian?'

*CHI: 我　　要　　　抱　　小　　　鸽子。
　　　Wǒ　yào　　bào　xiǎo　gēzi.
　　　I　　want to　hold　little　pigeon
　　　'I want to hold the little pigeon.'

*GRF: 小　　鸽子　　愿　　不　愿意　　让　你　　抱?
　　　Xiǎo　gēzi　yuàn　bú　yuànyì　ràng　nǐ　bào?
　　　little　pigeon　willing　not　willing　let　you　hold
　　　'Is the little pigeon willing to be held by you or not? '

*CHI: 愿意。
　　　Yuànyì.
　　　willing

'(It's) willing (to be held by me).'

*CHI: 它　多　　高兴　　啊！

Tā　duō　gāoxìng　a!

it　very　happy　P

'It is very happy!'

%act: 开始抓小鸽子 (starting to grab the little pigeon)

7. 能 *néng*

The first five deontic modal 能 *néng* 'can' utterances

i. (The child is drawing. Mommy helps her to hold the paper, but the child pushes mommy's hand away) D 1; 10.22

*MOT: 妈妈　　不　能　　扶？

Māma　bù　néng　fú?

mommy　not　can　hold

'Mommy can not hold (the paper)?'

*CHI: 妈妈　　能　扶。

Māma　néng　fú.

mommy　can　hold

'Mommy can hold (the paper).'

%act: 把妈妈的手放回到画纸上 (putting mommy's hand back to the paper)

ii. & iii. (Mommy bought a cake for the child's second birthday) V 2; 0.02

*CHI: 妈妈　　不　能　　吃　蛋糕。

Māma　bù　néng　chī　dàngāo.

mommy　not　can　eat　cake

'Mommy can not eat the cake.'

*MOT: 妈妈　　为什么　不　能　　吃　啊？

Māma　wèishénme　bù　néng　chī　a?

mommy　why　not　can　eat　P

'Why can not mommy eat the cake?'

*CHI: 妈妈　　　不　能　　吃　　蛋糕。

Māma　　bù　néng　chī　dàngāo.

mommy　not can　eat　cake

'Mommy can not eat the cake.'

*MOT: 妈妈　　　买　的。

Māma　　mǎi　de.

mommy　buy　P

'Mommy bought (it).'

*CHI: 妈妈　　　不　能　　的。

Māma　　bù　néng　de.

mommy　not　can　EMP

'Mommy can not (eat the cake)!'

iv. (The child wants to drink more milk. Mommy forbids her to do that) D 2; 0.26

*CHI: 不　　能　　　喝　　奶　　了。

Bù　néng　hē　nǎi　le.

not　can　drink　milk　PHA

'(I) can not drink milk.'

*CHI: 屁屁　红。

Pìpi　hóng.

ass　red

'(My) ass (may become) red.'

*CHI: 芊芊　　　喝　　水。

QiānQian　hē　shuǐ.

QianQian　drink　water

'Qian Qian (will) drink water.'

@Comment: 芊芊喝奶多了会上火，屁屁就会变红 (Qian Qian may have internal heat if she drinks too much milk, and as a result her ass will usually turn red.)

v. (It starts to rain. Daddy goes out to send mommy an umbrella. The child walks towards the doorway) D 2; 1.05

*CHI: 不　　能　　　出去。

Bù　　néng　　chūqù.

not　　can　　go out

'(I) can not go out.'

%act: 站在门口 (standing at the doorway)

The first five dynamic modal 能 *néng* 'can' utterances

i. (The child saw a butterfly, and wants to catch it) D 1; 11.04

*MOT: 芊芊　　能　不　能　　抓住?

Qiān Qian néng bù　néng　zhuāzhù?

Qian Qian can　not can　　catch

'Can you catch (it), Qian Qian? '

*CHI: 不　　能。

Bù　　néng.

not　　can

'(I) can not (catch it).'

*MOT: 那　　算了。

Nà　　suànle.

then　forget it

'Then forget it.'

*MOT: 让　　蝴蝶　　自由地　飞　吧。

Ràng húdié　zìyóude fēi　ba.

let　butterfly freely　fly　P

'Let the butterfly fly freely.'

ii. (The child hided tissue paper under the pillow) D 1; 11.14

*MOT: 妈妈　　能　不　能　　找到?

Māma　néng bù　néng　zhǎodào?

mommy can　not can　　find

'Can mommy find (it)?'

*CHI: 不　能　　找到。

　　　Bù　néng　zhǎodào.

　　　not can　　find

　　　'(Mommy) can not find (it).'

iii. (The child asks daddy to buy a pair of skating shoes for her) D 1; 11.29

*CHI: 芊芊　　　滑　　不　动。

　　　Qiān Qian　huá　bú　dòng.

　　　Qian Qian　skate　not　move

　　　'Qian Qian can not skate.'

*CHI: 能　　滑　　　动。

　　　Néng　huá　　dòng.

　　　can　　skate　move

　　　'(I) can skate.'

iv. (The child goes out to play with her aunt) D 2; 0.26

*ZHA: 芊芊　　　累　　了　　吧?

　　　QiānQian　lèi　le　　ba?

　　　Qian Qian tired　PHA　P

　　　'Are you tired, Qian Qian?'

*ZHA: 姑姑　　抱　　你　　吧?

　　　GūGu　bào　nǐ　　ba?

　　　aunt　hold　you　P

　　　'Shall aunt hold you?'

*CHI: 我　　能　　　跑。

　　　Wǒ　néng　pǎo.

　　　I　　can　　run

　　　'I can run.'

v. (The child is trying to climb up the wall) D 2; 1.13

*MOT: 你　　能　　不　　能　　爬　　上去?

Nǐ　néng　bù　néng　pá　shàngqù?

you　can　not　can　climb　up

'Can you climb up (the wall)?'

*CHI: 能。

Néng.

can

'(I) can (climb up the wall).'

*MOT: 我　　不　　信。

Wǒ　bú　xìn.

I　not　believe

'I do not believe (it).'

*CHI: 爬　　不　　动。

Pá　bú　dòng.

climb　not　move

'(I) can not climb up.'

*CHI: 老　　了。

Lǎo　le.

old　PHA

'(I'm) old.'

%act: 停止往墙上爬 (ceased climbing up the wall)

8. 可以 kěyǐ

The first five deontic modal 可以 kěyǐ 'may' utterances

i. (The child is playing with the building blocks) V 1; 11.22

*FAT: 汪汪　　带　　走　　可　　不　　可以?

Wāngwang　dài　zǒu　kě　bù　kěyǐ?

doggy　take　away　may　not　may

'May I take the doggy away?'

*CHI: 可以。

Kěyǐ.

may　　　　　　．

'(You) may (take the doggy away).'

%act: 继续玩积木 (going on playing with the building blocks)

ii. (The child takes away mommy's CD box) D 2; 0.02

*MOT: 芊芊　　 这个　 不　 可以　 拿。

　　　 QiānQian zhège bù kěyǐ ná.

　　　 Qian Qian this　 not　 may　 take

　　　 'You can not take this, Qian Qian.'

%act: 拿回 CD 盒子 (taking back the CD box)

*CHI: 拿　 这个　 可以　 吧?

　　　 Ná zhège kěyǐ ba?

　　　 take　 this　 may　 P

　　　 'May (I) take this?'

%act: 拿了妈妈的本子 (taking away mommy's notebook)

iii. (The child turns to climb up the bed while she is having breakfast) D 2; 1.01

*GRF: 吃　 饭　 去。

　　　 Chī fàn qù.

　　　 eat　 meal　 go

　　　 'Go to have your meal.'

*GRF: 去　 穿　 上　 鞋。

　　　 Qù chuān shàng xié.

　　　 go　 put　 on　 shoe

　　　 'Go to put on your shoes.'

*CHI: 穿　 上　 鞋　 可以　 了。

　　　 Chuān shàng xié kěyǐ le.

　　　 put　 on　 shoe　 may　 P

　　　 '(I) may (climb up the bed after I) put on the shoes.'

*GRF: 穿　 上　 鞋　 也　 不　 能　 上　 床　 吃　 饭。

　　　 Chān shàng xié yě bù néng shàng chuáng chī fàn.

put   on   shoe still not   can   climb   bed   eat   meal
'You may not eat sitting on bed even after (you have) put
on your shoes.'

iv. (Mommy bathes the child) D 2; 1.03

*CHI: 洒　　　这个　　可以　　吧?
Sǎ　　zhège　kěyǐ　ba?
sprinkle   this   may   P
'May I sprinkle (water with) this?'
%act: 拿了一个能洒水的玩具 (grabbing a toy that can hold and
sprinkle water)

v. (Grandma lies down and is ready to go to sleep) D 2; 1.07

*CHI: 我　　躺　　可以　　吧?
Wǒ　tǎng　kěyǐ　ba?
I　　lay　　may　　P
'May I lie down?'
%act: 躺在奶奶身旁 (lying down besides grandma)

The first five dynamic modal 可以 kěyǐ 'can' utterances

i. (The child takes a pen and starts to draw on a piece of paper.
The pen is out of ink. The child takes another pen) D 2; 1.02

*CHI: 这个　　可以。
Zhège kěyǐ.
this   can
'This pen works.'

ii. (The child tries on her shoes) D 2; 1.02

*CHI: 这个　鞋　　不　　烂。
Zhège xié　bú　làn.
this   shoe   not   worn
'This shoe is not worn.'

*CHI: 姑姑　买　　的。

Gūgu　mǎi　de.

aunt　buy　P

'Aunt bought (it for me).'

*CHI: 奶奶　　买　　的。

Nǎinai　mǎi　de.

grandma　buy　P

'Grandma bought (it for me).'

*CHI: 婆婆　　买　　的。

Pópo　mǎi　de.

grandma　buy　P

'Grandma bought (it for me).'

*CHI: 这个　鞋　可以　穿。

Zhège　xié　kěyǐ　chuān.

this　shoe　can　wear

'This shoe can be worn.'

iii. (The child asks daddy to take her to swim) D 2; 1.04

*CHI: 戴　游泳圈，　芊芊　可以　游泳　了。

Dài　yóuyǒngquān, QiānQiān　kěyǐ　yóuyǒng　le.

put on swing ring　Qian Qian　can　swim　PHA

'Qian Qian can swim with a swim ring.'

iv. (The child asks daddy to buy a motorcycle) D 2; 1.10

*FAT: 买　一　个　摩托车　　干　什么？

Mǎi　yī　gè　mótuōchē　gàn　shénme?

buy　one PL　motorcycle　do　what

'Why to buy a motorcycle?'

*CHI: 我　可以　坐　了。

Wǒ　kěyǐ　zuò　le.

I　can　sit　PHA

'I can sit (on it).'

v. (Daddy pushes the child up a tree) D 2; 1.10

*CHI: 芊芊　　　可以　　爬　　树　　了。
　　　 QiānQian　 kěyǐ　 pá　 shù　 le.
　　　 Qian Qian can　　climb tree PHA
　　　 'Qian Qian can climb up the tree.'

*CHI: 妈妈　　　　撵　　不　　　上。
　　　 Māma　　 niǎn　 bù　 shàng.
　　　 mommy　 catch　 not　 up
　　　 'Mommy can not catch up (me).'

9. 该 gāi

The first five deontic modal 该 gāi 'should' utterances

i. (Daddy hold the child in his arms and go back home from outside.) D 1; 11.29

*CHI: 该　　　吃饭　　了。
　　　 Gāi　　 chīfàn　 le.
　　　 should eat　　 PHA
　　　 'It's time to eat.'

ii. (The child is playing her building block) D 2; 0.10

*MOT: 明天　　　玩?
　　　 Míngtiān　 wán?
　　　 tomorrow　 play
　　　 '(Will you) play with it tomorrow?'

*CHI: 装　　　起来,　装　　　起来。
　　　 Zhuāng　 qǐlái,　 zhuāng　 qǐlái.
　　　 load　 in　　 load　 in
　　　 'Put (these) in (the box). Put (these) in (the box).'

*CHI: 都　　是　　积木,　　　都　　是　　积木。
　　　 Dōu　 shì　 jīmù,　　 dōu　 shì　 jīmù.
　　　 all　 are building block all　 are　 building block

'All are building blocks.'

*CHI: 该　　　　收　　　起来　　　了。
　　　Gāi　　shōu　　qǐlái　　le.
　　　should　load　in　　　PHA
　　　'It's time to put (these) in (the box).'

iii. (Mommy and the child are talking while lying in bed) D 2; 0.30

*CHI: 该　　　睡觉　　　了。
　　　Gaī　　shuìjiào　le.
　　　should　sleep　　PHA
　　　'It's time to sleep.'

iv. (The child has just had her milk. Mommy holds her in the arms.) D 2; 1.01

*CHI: 吃　　饱　　了。
　　　Chī　bǎo　le
　　　Eat　full　PHA
　　　'I'm full now.'

*CHI: 该　　　睡觉　　　了。
　　　Gāi　　shuìjiào　le.
　　　should　sleep　　PHA
　　　'It's time to go to sleep.'

v. (The child holds aunt's watch in her hand, and tries to tell the time) D 2; 1.03

*CHI: 七、　八、　十。
　　　Qī　　bā　　shí.
　　　seven　eight　ten
　　　'Seven (o'clock), eight (o'clock), ten (o'clock).'

%act: 看着姑姑的手表 (looking at aunt's watch)

*CHI: 该　　　吃饭　　了。
　　　Gāi　　chīfàn　le.

should eat PHA

'It's time to eat.'

The first five epistemic modal 该 *gāi* 'should' utterances

i. (The child saw her aunt grabbed the cup and umbrella as she usually had been doing before going to the library) D 2; 1.03

*CHI: 姑姑　　该　　　走　　了。

Gūgu gāi zǒu le.

aunt should leave PHA

'Aunt should be leaving.'

ii. (The child is playing with mother) D 2; 1.09

*CHI: 不　　叫　　吃饭。

Bú jiào chīfàn.

not let eat

'Not let (mommy) eat.'

*CHI: 妈妈　　　该　　哭。

Māma gāi kū.

mommy will cry

'Mommy should cry.'

iii. (Daddy is playing with the child. The child asks daddy to take off his jacket as he usually does, while daddy refuses to take it off) D 2; 1.10

*CHI: 爸爸　　不　　脱　　　衣服。

Bàba bù tuō yīfu.

daddy not take off clothes

'Daddy will not take off his clothes.'

*CHI: 爸爸　　该　　　走　　了。

Bàba gāi zǒu le.

daddy should leave PHA

'Daddy should be leaving.'

iv. (The child forbids grandpa from eating her food.) D 2; 1.13

*CHI: 虫子　　咬　　咬　　咬　（爷爷的　　肚子）。
　　　Chóngzi　yǎo　yǎo　yǎo　（yéyede　dùzi）.
　　　worm　bite　bite　bite　（grandpa's　belly)
　　　'Worm (may) bite (grandpa's belly).'

*CHI: 爷爷　　　该　　叫唤　　了。
　　　Yéye　gāi　jiàohuàn　le.
　　　grandpa　should　yell　PHA
　　　'Grandpa should yell.'

v. (Grandpa has a towel on his shoulder.) D 2; 1.25

*CHI: 姥爷　　该　　洗脸　　了。
　　　Lǎoye　gāi　xǐliǎn　le.
　　　grandpa　should　wash face　PHA
　　　'Grandpa should wash his face.'

10. 得 děi

The first five deontic modal 得 děi 'have to' utterances

i. (The child slips on the wet floor) D 2; 2.03

*CHI: 得　　小心　　点。
　　　Děi　xiǎoxīn　diǎn.
　　　have to　careful　a little
　　　'(I) have to be careful.'

ii. (It has just rained.) D 2; 3.01

*CHI: 我　得　　小心　　点。
　　　Wǒ　děi　xiǎoxīn　diǎn.
　　　I　have to　careful　a little
　　　'I have to be careful.'

%act: 去操场 (walking to the playground)

iii. (The child is playing house with the doll, and pretends she is the doll's mommy.) V 2; 4.12

*CHI: 她　　还　　得　　　　擦　　屁屁。
　　　Tā　hái　děi　　cā　　pìpi.
　　　she　still　have to　wipe　ass
　　　'(I) still have to wipe (the shit off her) ass. '

iv. (The child is playing with grandma) D 2; 5.13

*GRM: 我　　想　　让　　你　　跟　　我　　玩儿。
　　　Wǒ　xiǎng　ràng　nǐ　gēn　wǒ　wán'er.
　　　I　want　let　you　with　me　play
　　　'I want you to play with me.'
*CHI: 我　不　想　　跟　　你　　玩儿　了。
　　　Wǒ　bù　xiǎng　gēn　nǐ　wán'er　le.
　　　I　not　want　with　you　play　P
　　　'I do not want to play with you.'
*CHI: 我　　得　　　　上班。
　　　Wǒ　děi　　shàngbān.
　　　I　have to　go to work
%act: 假装去上班了 (pretending to go to work)

v. (Daddy talks with the child about the decision to send her to kindergarten later) D 2; 5.27

*CHI: 老师　　光　　　批评。
　　　Lǎoshī　guāng　pīpíng.
　　　teacher　will　criticize
　　　'The teacher will criticize me.'

*CHI: 我　　得　　　　上学　　　去。
　　　Wǒ　děi　　shàngxué　qù.
　　　I　have to　go to school　go
　　　'I have to go to school.'

The first five dynamic modal 得 *děi* 'need' utterances

i. (Mommy lets the child drink some water in the morning. Otherwise she might have a stomachache and needs to take medicine.) D 2; 2.08

*CHI: 肚肚　　　xx,　得　　吃　　药。
      Dùdu　　xx,　*děi*　*chī*　*yào.*
      stomach　xx,　　must　have　medicine
      'If stomach xx, (I) must have medicine.'

ii. (Grandma goes to the kitchen to have some food) D 2; 4.04

*CHI: 我　　得　　吃　　饭。
      Wǒ　*děi*　　*chī*　*fàn.*
      I　　　must　eat　　food
      'I must eat.'
%act: 跟着婆婆 (following grandma)

iii. (The child is trying to make the doll sit straight, while the doll can not sit straight by itself) V 2; 4.04

*CHI: 它　　非得　要　　歪。
      Tā　*fēiděi*　*yào*　　*wāi.*
      it　　must　want　askew
      'It must (sit) askew.'

iv. (Grandma takes a bottle of water before going out for a walk) D 2; 4.19

*CHI: 我　　生病　　　了。
      Wǒ　*shēngbìng*　*le.*
      I　　sick　　　PHA
      'I'm sick.'
*CHI: 得　　喝　　药。
      Děi　*hē*　　*yào.*
      must　drink　medicine

'(I) must have some medicine.'
%act: 指着水 (pointing to the water)

@Comment: 芊芊明知道瓶子里是水，她假装水是药 (Qian Qian knows there is water inside the bottle, and she said it contained medicine only to play house with herself.)

v. (The child is eating cookies) D 2; 5.25

*CHI: 吃　　　饼　　　光　　　上火。
　　　 Chī　 bǐng　 guāng　 shànghuǒ.
　　　 eat　 cookies　 will　 have internal heat
　　　 'Eating cookies will (make me) have internal heat.'
*CHI: 我　　得　　喝　　点　　奶。
　　　 Wǒ　 děi　 hē　 diǎn　 nǎi.
　　　 I　　 must　 drink some　 milk
　　　 'I must drink some milk.'

11. 喜欢 xǐhuan

The first five dynamic modal 喜欢 xǐ huan 'like' utterances

i. (The child holds the doll in her arms, and pets it gently.) V 2; 4.12

*GRM: 摸摸　　它　　吧。
　　　 Mōmo　 tā　 ba.
　　　 pet　　 it　 P
　　　 'Pet it.'
*CHI: 我　 xx #　喜欢　　# 摸摸　它。
　　　 Wǒ　 xx #　 xǐhuān #　 mōmo　 tā.
　　　 I　　 xx #　 like to　 # pet　 it
　　　 'I xx # like to pet it.'

ii. (The child is playing house with herself, and pretends to wash her face with leaves.) D 2; 6.18

*CHI: 芊芊　　　是个　好　孩子, 喜欢　　洗　　脸。
　　　Qiān Qian shì ge hǎo háizi, xǐhuān xǐ liǎn.
　　　Qian Qian is PL good kid, like to wash face
　　　'Qian Qian is a good kid, (since she) likes to wash face.'

iii. (The child wants to put on mommy's high-heel shoes, while mommy forbids her from doing that.) D 2; 6.18

*CHI: 我　喜欢　　穿　　你的　　高跟鞋。
　　　Wǒ xǐhuān chuān nǐde gāogēnxié.
　　　I like to wear your high-heel shoe
　　　'I like to wear your high-heel shoes.'

iv. (The child climbs the pole on bed, and claims that she is a little monkey.) D 2; 7.24

*FAT: 小猴子　　　喜欢　　　干　什么？
　　　Xiǎohóuzi xǐhuān gàn shénme?
　　　little monkey like to do what
　　　'What does little monkey like to do?'

*CHI: 喜欢　　爬　　这个　杆。
　　　Xǐhuān pá zhège gān.
　　　like to climb this pole
　　　'(It) likes to climb this pole.'

v. (The child is playing house with mommy, and pretends to cook for mommy.) V 2; 10.01

*CHI: 你　喜欢　　吃　辣椒饭　　　　　吗？
　　　Nǐ xǐhuān chī làjiāofàn ma.
　　　you like to eat cayennepepper meal P
　　　'Do you like to have cayennepepper meal?'

作者简介

杨贝，女，1979 年 7 月生，汉族，副教授，现任教于广东外语外贸大学。2010 年获得广东外语外贸大学外国语言学及应用语言学博士学位，2013 年在美国哈佛大学从事博士后研究一年。研究领域为应用语言学，研究兴趣包括：母语习得、二语习得、学习者语料库研究，先后发表论文 12 篇，出版专著 1 部。

专著：

《汉语儿童情态动词早期习得研究》，科学出版社，2014，独立

主要学术论文：

1. 现代汉语情态动词早期习得的个案研究，《外国语》， 2014（1），第一。

2. 汉语儿童认识型情态动词的早期习得，《语言教学与研究》，2014（1），独立。

3. 汉语动力型情态动词的早期获得，《华文教学与研究》，2013（1），第一。

4. 奎因难题与儿童词汇习得理论，《外语教学与研究》，2011（4），独立。被《中国社会科学文摘》2011（12）转载。

5. 走近学习驱动数据——数据驱动学习的延伸，《广东外语外贸大学学报》，2010（3），独立。

6. 学生课堂展示在研究生英语教学中的作用，《国外外语教学》，2006（3），独立。

7. 中国英语学习者与本族语者并列连词用法对比研究，收录于《基于 CLEC 语料库的中国学习者英语分析》，主编：杨惠中、桂诗春、杨达复，上海外语教育出版社，2005，独立。

8. 中国英语学习者与本族语学生写作中 HAVE 用法比较，《外语教学》，2003（2），独立。